KASRA FARMANESH

WOMAN, LIFE, FREEDOM

novum ⬖ pro

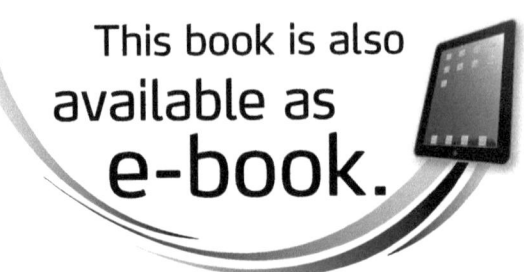

This book is also available as e-book.

© 2024 novum publishing

ISBN 978-3-99146-759-5
Editing: Samantha Acker
Cover design, layout & typesetting: novum publishing
Translated by: L. F.

Despite all efforts, the author has not succeeded in locating all copyright holders of the images. Therefore, please contact the publisher if any remuneration is due.

www.novum-publishing.co.uk

Print product with financial
climate contribution
ClimatePartner.com/16547-2311-1001

CONTENTS

PREFACE

Feeling both happiness and sorrow at the same time is one of the strange emotional combinations of humans, as well as being simultaneously happy for achieving a goal and being sad for the price you paid for accomplishing that. To achieve the goals of the "Woman, Life, Freedom" revolution, the best Iranians and the most free-spirited and enlightened people risked their lives and jeopardized everything. Dealing with their story and paying attention to their revolutionary movement fills the hearts of every person with sorrow and enthusiasm.

The purity, genuineness, depth, and glory of the Iranian movement, and forerunners of the "Woman, Life, Freedom" revolution, created a human and social responsibility for all of us because the point and the content of this movement are aimed at all Iranians. This revolution is a process that'll change one thing – and that is everything. This book, **Woman, Life, Freedom**, announces a historical and expressive disagreement against the culture of political and religious oppression, which has hindered the growth and development of Iranian society from the past to the present.

The Iranians' battle is against regressed and petrified devils who have held hostages of their own sect's and group's illusions. I believe that to achieve human freedom, freer humans must make sacrifices. So, let me remind you of the eternal hero of the freedom path, Artin Rahmani, the 16-year-old teenager who wrote, *"Mother, I'm sorry. I want to take a step in a way that you may not see my youth"*, before beginning his fight. He loved living but sacrificed himself for this glorious goal. He passed through his own life and gave life to others. Separating deliberately from his mother, expressed through a feeling of shame, is not even understandable and describable. Artin bid farewell to the best and most important person in his life to achieve the best for Iranians.

In a world where the smallest and least possessions are being protected, the separation of a teenager from his mother means giving up everything he has. Feeling concern and anxiety for someone, who is the most valuable thing in his life, and war, simultaneously, against the Iranian nation's kidnappers and hostage takers, with the aim of freedom for Iranians, requires a strong motivation and a clear objective. He and the fighters of the path of freedom have translated and interpreted the most valuable and sacrificial states of human beings.

Writing and speaking about the heroes of freedom and democracy path, and then describing their sacrifices and noble ideals, is both heartbreaking and necessary. This article is a theoretical analysis of the "Woman, Life, Freedom" revolution. It is a description of the appearance and content of Iranians' uprising against a regime that represents ignorance and madness.

A political and religious system that has imprisoned the people of a land within the confines of their sick demarcation based on ideological beliefs describes what the visionary young people were struggling against to make a better future for everyone who made for and came from the future. It is a description of the people who have rebelled against frozen traditions in history and traditional people. It is obvious that such an event has been so immense that every speech and text will refer to a part of it, but our effort is to provide a clear and explicit analysis of the concepts of this movement.

Any efforts that were made toward the greatness and pride of the Iranian nation are really nothing, which is why I'm ashamed to even dedicate this article to the heroes of the "Woman, Life, Freedom" revolution.

I must pay my respects to some people, like Nika, Khodanor, Mahsa, Sarina, Siavash, Majidreza Rahnavard, Toomaj Salehi, and the unnamed, the deceased, and the prisoners, and anyone else that has had to suffer from torture.

Woman, Life, Freedom
By: Kasra Farmanesh

THE THEATER OF CULTURAL RELATIVISM

A 22-year-old girl named Mahsa Amini was murdered by the Islamic regime's morality police, also known as the Guidance Patrol, which caused the Iranians' blood to boil. Mahsa was arrested by the police due to not fully adhering to the mandatory hijab, and, during her arrest and while she was in the detention center, she was insulted, brutally beaten, and subjected to violence, which resulted in her death. What happened to Mahsa caused a national uproar as Iranians saw their own living conditions in the plight of the Iranian girl. She was like a mirror in which every Iranian saw themselves. Her death became a symbol of the suffocating atmosphere experienced by every Iranian. Her death was like a trigger for the outflowing of hatred that Iranians have always carried with them.

Iranians' disgust of the Islamic regime had existed before Mahsa's death and continued, like an underlying reality hidden under the skin. But it was always special occasions and incidents that unify the nation. As a result, those cause the roar and action of citizens. The people's lack of reaction and temporary silence, which is just a consequence of facing weapons and the regime's military tools, does not imply acceptance or endorsement of imposed conditions in any part of the world. The existence and continuation of governments do not necessarily mean that they have the people's support. The silence of Iranians in some periods has been strategic rather than supportive. They have just been waiting for an opportunity to express their dissatisfaction and disgust with the Islamic regime.

The political and social silence of individuals can sometimes mean their approval and satisfaction with the conditions, or that it is full of unvoiced protests and discontent in which circumstances and situations don't allow them to be expressed. Such silence is obligatory and imposed. In the face of imposed silence, there is always the possibility of an explosion of inner feelings and suppressed desires.

The people's protests, when faced with the tragic death of Mahsa, were a manifestation and explosion of their deep discontent with society's brutal behavior of the Islamic regime toward Iranians and women. Protests against the horrible death of the Saqqezian girl are not limited to Mahsa but have encompassed many 'Mahsas'. She was a symbol of oppressed Iranian women and of the population's oppression, in general, and humiliation of their human dignity.

She represents the Mullahs' imposed suffocation and the unfree Iranian society. All Iranians saw themselves as victims of the Islamic regime with the slight toward Mahsa and her heartbreaking plight. Mahsa Amini's character embodied the historical oppression and discrimination experienced by Iranians.

Mahsa was Iran, and Iran was Mahsa.

Thus, Iranians around the country from north to south and east to west, in different ethnic groups, and with different political and ideological attitudes, found a common ground, which let them unite and start an integrated revolution against the totalitarian regime. It was a revolution against the common enemy for a common objective. It was a revolution against the zombies who fed on the lives and possessions of the people.

There was an uprising against the Mullahs, rulers, and Islamic Revolutionary Guard terrorists, who are enemies of every Iranian. It was against the foreigners who destroyed the structure and foundation of society and ruined and pushed a historically proud nation toward decline and destruction every day. It was against the ruling elites that their habit of spreading death and destruction dust on young men's hopes and futures. The decision to remove the Islamic regime and the guardianship of Islamic jurists as a common enemy of the people was a common desire that united the Iranian nation. The feelings of disgust from the Islamic regime and demands for change were a common desire in the minds and hearts of Iranians. This demand brought people closer to each other and stronger.

On the other hand, having common goals was the second strengthening factor that doubled the cohesion of Iranians.

Women's rights, liberalism, equality, democracy, and human rights were among the central principles and demands of the revolution of "Woman, Life, Freedom".

Iranians knew exactly what they were denying and fighting for. The starting point and ultimate goal of the Iranian uprising were both clear. The cohesive and freedom-seeking mentality of Iranians also made many cultural and political critics somewhat baffled and shocked.

Those who believed that Iran's geopolitical and territorial borders in the Middle East justified tyranny were convinced that Iranians, living there, were Islamists and traditionalists whose beliefs contradicted the concept of democracy.

But the surprising intellectual and revolutionary storm of Iranians, especially the younger generation, was so terrible and unexpected that it shocked the enlightened part of Iranian society as well as the global community. Their slogans and demands were different and distinct from what many expected. Some considered their slogans irrelevant to the people of the Middle East and fundamentally denied the existence of such mentalities and goals there.

Some analysts and politicians, using the concept of cultural relativism (also beloved by dictators and oppressors), have ignored the human rights violations in Iran, the Middle East, and some Eastern countries. They used the excuse *"We in the West have liberal and democratic values that belong to us, while they are in the East, where misogyny and oppression are part of their culture"* to justify their inaction and conservatism.

They claimed that if people in the West enjoy individual and civil rights as a common and popular culture, then it is due to the Western people's choice; while, if tradition and religion have power in the Middle East, then it is due to their own lifestyle choice. From these beliefs, they concluded that supporting or paying attention to the politics and social situations of countries was not in line with global standards of human values.

I have always believed that those nonsense beliefs and justifications can have just two assumptions: either they live in a layer of wholly wrong and abstract understanding and express incorrect and fallacious views due to ignorance, or they intentionally close their eyes to the truth and correct position to justify their inaction and to deliberately avoid responsibility and duty since admitting the truth is somehow incurring new responsibilities and is a limiting act.

The Iranian people showed the emptiness of these claims quite powerfully and visibly. These kinds of invalidations of ideas are the most explicitly convincing model for rejecting a claim. Iranians expressed in action that many of the theorists and analysts from both the East and the West have a background of fallacies and mistakes because their thoughts and ideas have no connection to the reality outside their minds and have no relevance to the social reality.

Sareena Esmailzadeh, a 16-year-old girl, is a deceased hero of this revolution, who was active on various social media platforms.

In one of her videos, she said:

"Iranian teenagers are aware of world conditions and ask themselves, 'What do we have less than an American teenager whose concerns are so different?'"

Such a statement's meaning is the announcement of the end of the theater of cultural relativism.

There is no difference between me and Esmailzadeh. There is no distinction between us and them. We have equal needs and require common answers. The types of border and territorial structures do not determine my imprisonment and her freedom. In the same way, they were not like this and became what we want to be so we will become so. 'Becomings' are the same, but there is a difference in time, obstacles, and factors. The goals are the same, but some people respond sooner than others to their needs, rights, and desires, due to special conditions. This process does not deprive anyone and does not give an inherent advantage to others.

However, since many analysts and theorists analyze and think based on an abstract repository of concepts, the Iranian people's uprising somehow shook their minds and told them that sleepers must wake up from their pseudo-intellectualism and dogmatic dreams. If one is a citizen of the United States, France, or Britain, they are no different from the one who lives in the Middle East.

If all the people of Earth have the same physiological and biological needs, such as for food, health, and medical care, they also have equal cultural and legal needs, like the right to freedom of speech and beliefs, the preservation of human dignity and value, the right to choose their clothes, and the right to choose their desired lifestyle. Some people do not hesitate or doubt the sameness of humans' biological needs, but they do resist and struggle against cultural and legal rights. This monopoly of the dedication of certain rights to some humans at a specific geographical location and the simultaneous exclusion and deprivation of other groups through pseudo-philosophical justifications at another place on Earth is unjustified discrimination among humans.

No culture or thought is limited within the borders of geographic territories. Negating this relativity does not mean denying the differences. Freedom of expression is not exclusive to Americans, and censorship is not just of Chinese heritage. The political conditions and suffocation imposed by parties and groups can't mislead the rights and needs of humans, even if citizens feel somewhat self-alienated and consider slavery as their right.

The "Woman, Life, Freedom" revolution is a secular movement, both politically and philosophically. From the heart of a country whose name has been repeated with an Islamic suffix, many questions come to the surface:

Where were these democrats, freedom-seekers, and this generation educated?

Did anyone teach them political and sociological philosophy?

How did they find the distance between themselves from their previous generation so far?

How and with which process do they bravely and consciously say, "NO!" to entrenched traditions?

How was it possible to raise a leading and modern generation within the controlled political and educational system of the Mullahs?

How could the Islamic veil, which had been widely promoted and imposed, burn in the fire of anger and rationality of the young Iranian generation?

How did this level of democracy grow in their minds?

Where did the unique courage and bravery of Iranians against the tyranny of the regime come from?

Countless difficult questions constantly occupied the minds of observers, including outsiders, as other nations have always heard and seen lies or controlled parts of reality about the people and society of Iran, and, somehow, an unreal or incomplete image of Iranian society has been reported to them. The media had inverted or selected facts and realities and depicted them in a certain way. Some people in developed countries thought that a free lifestyle, democracy, and secularism were the only countries with the same features and conditions and that gender equality, secular democracy, and the rules of law were specific to Western societies. In other words, these modern concepts – unspoken and unwritten – were put in the minds of those populations. It was natural that there was no coherence and conformity between the misogynist fanatical Middle Eastern man and men who were shot and tortured in the streets and prisons to defend women's rights. They assumed that hijab, Islamism, traditionalism, and misogyny were among the accepted Iranian cultures, even though the behavior of governments and rulers did not represent the people's beliefs and demands. And even in democratic societies, all political behaviors and positions of a government do not reflect the people's views.

The argument, *Because the government is Islamic, therefore the people are also Islamic, or because the government represents Communism, therefore, the people are also Communist*, is incorrect and fallacious reasoning. Such a simple conclusion has been accepted by some parts of society. However, in a fully democratic society that adheres to the attributes of democracy, this reasoning is only partially reasonable and is not employed in an authoritarian and controlled society. Furthermore, using such judgments as the basis for determining differences among people and making divisions and inequalities is wholly misguided.

The belief, *If you are English, French, or American, then you are modern, and if you are Iranian, Turkish, or Chinese, then you are against modernity*, is a collective myth among certain groups of people around the world.

Reality is not a game played by politicians, who, through a mountain of fallacies and propaganda, seek to justify the status quo of countries using populist methods and techniques. The concepts of *truth* and *reality* are not determined based on geographical regions such as the East and West or North and South. The truth in the political, decision, and policymaking arena is determined based on the happiness, prosperity, and well-being of the humans and creatures affected by such decisions.

The truth is determined based on how people's words and beliefs align with reality.

For instance, if it is claimed that people in Eastern countries do not want freedom, democracy, or social ethics, that is not true because it does not align with reality.

Yes, there are cultural differences, but the differences do not mean that that culture is correct and relative. A wrong culture, which is due to the existence of governments, conditions, and suppression situations, has no reason for validity, judgment, and valuation.

All societies have experienced ups and downs and have always experienced positive and negative situations in various fields. Women's status and human rights in Europe may not have been much better than those in Eastern societies decades and centuries ago.

Have French and British women simply had the right to vote or did they have to achieve it?

Has gender equality always simply existed in Western culture and history, or has it been achieved through years of struggle?

Has the behavior of the Japanese always been like what it is today, being one of the best examples of order, respect, modernity, and civilization? The history of World War II and the horrific events carried out by Japanese soldiers and government forces are the opposite of the current image that people of the world have of this country.

Nowadays, Britain is considered a civilized and modern country, but has there been a more colonialist country like Britain throughout history? Has history witnessed a more imperialist political system like Britain's? The English have been robbing and looting from New Zealand and Australia to India, Canada, and America. The famous phrase *The sun never sets on the British Empire* is an expression of the extent of British aggression. In World War I, the Brits even occupied Iran, violating national sovereignty from the south and the Russians from the north. One of the main reasons for the great famine from 1917 to 1919, which killed millions of Iranians due to starvation, was the inhumane behavior of the occupiers.

Therefore, a country can't be considered to have specific inherent characteristics solely due to its current appropriate political and social situation. People from another country cannot be categorized as hostile and strangers to modern concepts solely due to their current imposed situation. If an Icelandic citizen were born in Saudi Arabia, they were very likely to be a Muslim. But if an Arab person was born in Iceland, they were unlikely to be a Muslim. Most of the features and traits that people see in themselves are the product of environmental factors ... an environment that will be determined by society, parents, and the political and economic system. Therefore, both the culture and current situation of an Icelandic or Norwegian person are created under completely fragile and arbitrary circumstances. An appropriate foundation and good educational conditions have been very decisive in determining behaviors and attitudes.

Despite that, if a group identifies these cultural and social traits to be exclusive to themselves and considers others unrelated to modernity and accuses them of being inherently traditional or religious, they have made an unfair judgment and presented an inaccurate description as a large part of their cultural wealth is borrowed or inherited from their environment and social conditions. If someone is in a different geographic location and is in undesirable conditions, they are influenced by the function of the environmental and social situations imposed on them.

A Chinese citizen under Communist rule is no different than a free American citizen enjoying a liberal democracy. Random events and causes have thrown each of them into a corner of the world. The point is that the American citizen has no right to label Chinese citizens, who are under oppression, as inferior. In an equal environment, the Chinese citizen may be much more liberal and progressive than the American citizen. Therefore, if someone tries to normalize the living conditions of the Chinese by making excuses and doling out unjustified ideas, called cultural relativity, they are actually pouring out their own unconsciousness or inner meanness in a conceptual and political framework. Just as a Briton needs freedom, so do a Korean and an Indian needs freedom. No one is separated or has more rights than others when we consider rights. Humans are equal and all have equal rights. The existence of a dictator and a sick system does not determine different rights for humans.

The next point is that cultural relativism, which means understanding the causes and factors that produce ideas and behaviors at the level of society, is not a subject that should be criticized now. But justifying discrimination and violating human and civil rights, while showing that suffocation is normal is wrong. Different customs and traditions are natural and not only have no problem, but they are also beauties that exist among different societies and nations. Customs and traditions may vary greatly between countries and cities because they are a function of history, tradition, nature, and personal interests.

The main issue is that human rights can't be subject to deletion or distortion under irrelevant justifications and explanations. If the majority of society demands the elimination of sexual minorities, then such a demand is not only illegitimate, but it is also not acceptable because the protection of minority rights is part of human and civil rights and is not dependent on the approval or disapproval of others. Therefore, even wrong general culture societies cannot eliminate or deprive human rights. The right to freely choose body coverings and clothes is also a part of human rights that derives from humans' ownership of their own bodies. It is not possible to justify compulsory hijab in a country under a cultural relativism pretext. Even if the majority of people want it, it still can't be legitimated because deciding on the type of dresses and clothes for individuals is beyond the scope of the decision-making process of the majority, and the interests of others can't be imposed. The right and wrong of every issue can't be determined by the majority's demands or beliefs.

Democracy is not necessarily about blindly obeying the majority in all subjects. Absolute imposition of the majority's views on minorities is the dictatorship of the masses. Minorities are one of the essential components of modern democracy because, before the majority, the human being is the criterion, and referring to the vote of the majority is to better administrate and fulfill human desires and rights.

This incorrect argument – if the majority of society is Muslim, then hijab should be mandatory – is also within the mentioned framework. However, it isn't clear if the majority of a society, like that in Iran, is Muslim or not. There aren't any accurate, scientific, or complete statistics available. Even if we assume that the majority of the society is Muslim, most Muslims may be secular in political views and may be against the government-imposed clothing and dressing rules. Moreover, even if they are not secular but agree with the imposition of hijab, they do not have the right to impose a specific style of dress on other citizens because they do not have the legal authority to implement such an act. This kind of behavior would be considered a violation of the rights and privacy of others and would be universally opposed, even if it is upholding the law and legislative system. These kinds of rules are basically invalid. Thus, opponents or minorities in such examples have the full right to dissent. However, such examples can't be applied to Iranian society because the people's rejection of political Islam is evident, and their opposition to legislation that is based on religious foundations can't be hidden.

However, in systems where minorities are forced to appear as the majority for the sake of having a free life, the concept of human rights and freedom will lose its meaning. This will be even more relevant in the case of a religious regime that seeks to impose its sectarian beliefs upon the majority of the people to make them self-alienated. Therefore, when human rights have such a powerful and unbreakable state, the justification and excuse, called cultural relativism, for normalizing situations with negative human rights in different countries will become clear.

REVOLUTION AND GENERATION Z

One of the important subjects that is quite evident in the "Woman, Life, Freedom" revolution is the breaking of taboos and false traditions and the rejection of anti-modernity symbols. This revolution is more cultural than political. The revolution entails overturning and transforming the form and content of the imposed culture or political structure. Therefore, the "Women, Life, Freedom" revolution is a fundamental and radical one. The issue is not just about changing the political system and potentially replacing a few politicians. Its content is about modernity and humanism, along with an anti-authoritarian attitude because, without such an attitude, changes in cultural and political diversity norms would not be possible.

As many new and pioneer generations in Iran are armed and equipped with the necessary intellectual tool, called critical thinking, they have the ability and power to overcome environmental determinism and the educational system. They have broken their own imposed belief system, and, by using analysis and processing, reevaluated everything that was imposed on them by obtaining the necessary information and knowledge from the depths of the censoring system of authorities. They have worked hard to destroy ingrained beliefs and reconstruct new ones. Those who were not initially influenced by the regime's media and propaganda have had an easier path to break down their beliefs. This mental and intellectual process was one of the foundations of the Iranians' uprising against the anti-modern beliefs and policies of the religious government. Those who seek to overthrow the religious government and establish a secular democracy have already broken down the prevailing beliefs in their minds and reconstructed new ideas. The courage and sense of awareness displayed on the streets of Iran, which inspired the U.S. President, were supported by humanism and awareness, rather than just political excitement or blind ignorance.

A remarkable event occurred amid a mass of religious and political restrictions. The people of Iran turned away from the government's political and ideological values, advertising, and the bombardment of information, and reproduced themselves. They tried to break free from the shackles of religion and tradition. They left obedience and abandoned the propaganda of the government. The difference between the beliefs of the people of a society and the beliefs of established governments is difficult to see because closed political systems represent public opinion in a similar way to what the system's desire is. This is a process that has not been solved for many citizens of the Western world in this third millennium. At times, due to the presence of the liberal government, politicians, and constitution, the number of liberal citizens has grown and developed. In other words, such citizens are passive liberals. If such citizens lived in a society with different values, they would conform to those values.

More than that, even citizens in free societies take a reverse path toward freedom and democracy, and take steps toward more restrictions, such as the repeal of the women's right to have an abortion and the defense of traditional and religious people in different parts of America from such reactionary laws. Meanwhile, a large section of society remains indifferent and silent in the face of such misguided legislation. This happened in the secure and liberal environment in America! Therefore, the importance and value of the people who moved toward freedom and democracy in the middle of immense restrictions, government advertising, and potential dangers become more apparent. That is why the "Woman, Life, Freedom" revolution is unique and a matter of pride and honor for Iranians. A citizen who has unconsciously accepted modern and liberal values in a suitable environment is not comparable to a self-made modern human.

Iranians are modernists who are trapped in the cage of religion and conservatism. They were the ones who displayed the world's first feminist revolution and did not give up on this endeavor. Therefore, many observed that citizens of developed countries admired the bravery and perseverance of Iranians and expressed their wonder. Many politicians also openly and officially acknowledged the extraordinary value and importance of the Iranian liberalism revolution. The Iranian people revolted against a religious and oppressive government while facing drastic economic and livelihood difficulties, but they carried out a revolution that was strongly liberal. It was not expected that a free and avant-garde revolution could be born within the complex and tragic economic situation. The courage and desire for the liberation of Iranians was exciting and shining. Everyday life problems and concerns did not make the Democrat and liberal people's movement insignificant or forgotten.

The Islamic regime believed that if they surrounded society and people with economic poverty and income inequality, then the idea of freedom and human rights would disappear from the public's mind. The regime did a comprehensive and continuous weakening of the people, making them economically and socially weaker, step by step, so they could focus all their attention on financial problems and providing basic life necessities for themselves and their families. The government's goal was to *forget about freedom when you are lacking food and money.* The government believed that if people's necessities of life, such as food, health, and housing, were endangered, and if people were constantly struggling to get those basic needs met, then they would not have the opportunity nor time to think about their social needs, self-actualization, progress, and development.

The leaders were unaware of the social and economic transitions and dissatisfaction that were taking place beneath the surface of Iranian society. At the same time, the circulation of information, communication, and the massive volume of data and speed of changes in the world were drawing thoughts in other directions. The Iranian people compared their living conditions and lifestyles – despite their endless efforts and life-long struggles to meet the necessities of life – to other people around the world.

Comparing several subjects is a way to understand differences, similarities, strengths, and weaknesses. Poverty and wealth, health and disease, prosperity and impoverished, progress and regression: each concept illustrates its opposite. Such a method is always going on in the daily lives of ordinary people, but when we consider the use of this method on a broader and more social level, it would lead us to the result. A comparison between the civil rights in developed and undeveloped countries, the level of social freedoms of modern and underdeveloped countries, and the level of political development of democratic and authoritarian countries. People not only use a comparison method in economic issues but also, through such measurements, discover the extent of the decrease of structures and laws in social and political issues.

The point is that the accuracy and quality of comparison depend on which tool and criteria are used. If I compare the behavior of 10 people in my daily life with superficial information, the result is limited to that number and size of data. The larger the amount of information and the breadth of comparison spectra, the more precise and reassuring the conclusion will be. In the new world, we are facing a wholly different issue that has turned the world into a small village, linking all humans in some way together and shining a light on hidden and dark angles.

Unknown areas, regions, and people are connected through the internet and social media. If, in history, suppression and elimination were prominent, then, in many cases, people did not know about the world around them because there were no tools for fast and documented information transfer. Their experience of seeing the world was likely limited to their birthplace, and they weren't able to experience different cities, and communities with different tastes, customs, and traditions. But, in the modern era, the fact that humans have access to such easy, fast, and free-to-use instruments becomes a nightmare for political criminals.

Facing the "Women, Life, Freedom" revolution in Iran, we are in front of a generation that significantly differs from those before it. These young people, known as Generation Z or, 'Zoomers', are the first generation to rebel against traditions and authoritarianism, plus they have a serious connection with the internet and social media networks. As our communication tools become stronger and broader, so too would these young people's information and experience. Today's youth have probably already experienced so many more different environments and people than a 90-year-old man, born decades ago, could even imagine.

In such an atmosphere, humans are constantly faced with contradictions between their own and others' possessions and also between their own and others' freedoms. These comparisons occur in all aspects of everyday life, from how individuals wear their clothes to the environmental conditions in different territories. These comparisons show either the superiority of a group over others or reveal deficiencies and weaknesses. To put it simply, either the lives and thoughts of individuals will be in a better state, or they will be faced with retardation and defects.

Iranians, especially the new, younger generation, have discovered, through comparison and matching, that they are living in the basement level of the global community, in the grip of a political system that has absolutely no understanding of humanism and democracy. It's a tyrannical regime that tries to control people by threat and force while, at the same time, observing the growth of democracy and levels of freedom in countries and lands around the world. They can observe the influence and value of a citizen's vote in the present and future of democratic societies, like how much political systems are influenced by citizen opinions and how much they depend on obtaining legitimacy from the people. By observing these differences, even a teenager understands his or her situation and that of others with complete clarity, leaving behind the confusion and disillusions instilled by the Islamic government and understanding that they are facing a storm of media lies and propaganda.

Comparison methods disgrace villainous executors and incapable political structures worldwide. That's why, in countries like North Korea, internet access and tools for communication, like social media, are strictly prohibited, as well as even reading and watching TV shows and movies. North Korean leaders know that their prisoners (the citizens) will perhaps want a different quality of life and way of living if they were to see images and texts beyond the Communist Party's propaganda. The leaders also know that their citizens will compare themselves to others and become aware of their tragic living situation, which may lead to increased dissatisfaction and a slow upheaval. They seek to control their citizens' bodies as well as their thoughts and beliefs, so no one can think differently (that their living conditions aren't good) when they are alone.

Illegitimate and inefficient governments and regimes put people's lives at risk and don't allow for any objections or other voices. Winston Churchill famously said, *"A weak economy has two reasons: Either rulers are stupid or fools rule. War and drought are excuses."* We experienced that in some countries such as Singapore and Japan, which have only a few significant natural resources and have achieved astonishing growth and development due to the proper management, rationality, and dynamic structures. In contrast, countries such as Venezuela and Iran, which are rich in natural resources, have fallen into a tourbillion of underdevelopment due to the stupidity and corruption of their leaders.

The defective political and economic structure of the Islamic government is one of the main reasons for the country's backwardness and underdevelopment. Amid thousands of layers of corruption and ignorance of the Mullahs' regime, nothing but ruins and destruction have been achieved, as a result. That's why the people of Iran, with incomparable natural resources and national wealth, are still struggling with countless problems. The Mullahs' method of management has caused Iran's lakes, wetlands, and rivers to dry up rapidly.

Desertification and deforestation are the results of the kleptocracy of corrupt managers who think only about the interests of their group, not anything else.

The Iranian people have observed the importance of climate and environmental issues for Western countries, while they see the indifference and lack of interest in this topic among the decision-makers in their own countries. When comparing their concerns and anxieties with people of developed countries, they feel deep despair about the effort, time, and energy required to own a vehicle, get married, or get medical treatment in their countries. Meanwhile, citizens of other countries, who may even be of the same age and same income level, have hardly any need to think about such issues.

People wonder why they must be in a place where they cannot experience well-being, freedom, and equality. What is the difference between me and young people in other countries? Why don't I have even the most basic rights, like choosing what to wear? Why is the government trying to control this issue, which is not even considered a topic in some countries, and turned it into such a social problem and tangled knot?

Why are, unlike all the countries in the world, Iranian women dictated to and forced to wear hijab, and it has to be a specific model of hijab, no less? Which country in the world has made hijab mandatory? There is no country other than the Islamic regime of Mullahs, which has become a bizarre and contradictory system and wants to imprison women. (Of course, the oppressed people of Afghanistan are experiencing a new Islamic regime that has started a competition with the Islamic regime in Iran in insanity.)

No one can answer the question: What is the ratio between me, a modern Iranian, and the arrogant retrograde Mullahs? Why should my body be a political platform for the clerics? With what license and approval has a Mullah made the lives of Iranians his playthings? Why is he the determiner of the lifestyles of a vast country's numerous people? Why is no one accountable for these countless questions? And why are people not allowed to question or object to anything?

Such a situation leads to thousands of visible and hidden questions that do not have answers because there are no answers.

A question that does not have a logical answer will make cruel persons and their subordinates illegitimate. As a result, the dictator will determine that dissent is not allowed, so the issue of accountability gets canceled automatically. Thousands of rightful demands and objections are prohibited. Thus, people feel like a volcano that is ready to erupt at any moment and tend to rebel against the political system. Tyrants imagine that they can control human minds like they control their bodies. They ignore the fact that the structure and function of the mind are different from the function of the body. Although blocking the path of information and knowledge is a mechanism to control citizens, it is not enough because the human mind is irrepressible and moving, and it can even contemplate beyond the prevailing trends in the most closed and isolated conditions.

Mullahs who demand absolute obedience of the people, even without adhering to their own self-defined and illegitimate responsibilities, are not accountable to any of the Iranians. They have not been accountable, and they also consider questions and objections to be crimes and offenses. They have placed themselves in a position where questioning them is also considered to be a crime and impudence. Such political chaos and disorder heavily affect citizens whose whole lives and futures are being influenced by the wrong decisions of these reckless Mullahs. Watching such a painful process every day becomes an irrecoverable hatred, an extreme hate of the agent and executor of this volume of harassment and meaningless impositions. The sharp-angled relationship between the Islamic regime and the people of Iran is one of hostility and elimination. Iranians do not recognize the regime as their representative, and the Islamic regime views the people of Iran as a threat to its slowly decreasing power. Both the Iranian regime and the people perceive the other as a threat to their survival and existence.

In such conditions, all responsibility for any unfortunate event that occurs falls on the Islamic government because the people have all the rights, and the illegitimate government and regime have none. Having all or no principles also has valid aspects.

One of them is the relationship between the people and the illegitimate political regime. People are authorized to use their rights in any appropriate form to achieve their desires. The entire country and both the political and management powers belong to the people, and the government has no share or right. Political systems, if they are legitimate and legal, obtain permission for political work and the management of the country from the people. Otherwise, there would be no difference between foreign occupiers, which has both political and legal implications. It does not mean that they do not have Iranian nationality (which is a superficial interpretation). It means that people are authorized to use every appropriate means and method to oppose and fight against any foreign occupiers.

People have rights, and systems have obligations. The determination of the system's obligations is related to the people. And the executors of such obligations are also determined by the people. On the other hand, different generations also define various responsibilities and policies for governments. A specific political version or model cannot be determined for everyone all the time. The fundamental issue is reflecting people's desires in the system of governance. In the case of Iran, there is no proportion between the desires and attitudes of Iranians and the rulers of the regime. The mindset and attitude of Generation Z have thousands of ideas, desires, and questions, and the Islamic government officials cannot even understand them, let alone respond to or implement them. The people of Iran had been staring at a horizon that the ideological minds of a handful of reactionary Mullahs and the suppressive terrorist military regime could not comprehend.

The people of Iran, especially the new generation, have no form of common awareness, or worldview, with the rulers of the Islamic regime and Mullahs. There are fundamental differences and disparities between the Islamic government and the Iranian people's opinions about the world, humanity, politics, and rights. Even the Iranian new generation's thinking methods have significant differences, which are specific to themselves compared to their previous generation. This is an indication of the concept of a Generational Gap, meaning the previous generation does not fully understand the current generation's intellectual system and beliefs because of life's complexities and more awareness in the modern world.

In some cases, each group lives in a separate and different world, mentally, while their bodies physically work, function, and coexist together.

This atmosphere intensely exists in Iran currently with a high level of differences. I believe that the younger generation of Iranians lives in a world in which, oftentimes, parents and previous generations cannot understand each other's priorities and needs. Even if they try, they may have access to a part of this world, but it may mean living together but separately. The human mind can create its own particular world, of which the person will be the director. In other words, individuals are usually the determinants of acceptable inputs and rejected outputs of such a world. So, the new generation creates their own world within a mental framework and model, attempting to enjoy their desired world, while the closest person in their lives cannot imagine it. If the new generation finds a statement or belief to be false, they will not believe in it, and if they recognize the correctness or validity of a belief or proposition, they will accept it. Force and threats are meaningless to them. Blind imitation and obedience are strange concepts for the new Iranian generation.

The human mind can continue its own desired game under the pressure of oppression without the fear of police or other repressor traditions. This person will eventually reveal his or her hidden thoughts and ideas because, in a specific situation, individuals will lose the ability to censor themselves due to pressure and imposed circumstances.

If living conditions and society do not allow the young people to live their chosen lifestyle or pursue their desired plans and goals, and if situations prohibit them from freely expressing their views on topics of their choosing, eventually such a deep difference will become apparent, and such an event will transform society fundamentally. The intensity of the changes will be rapid and incomprehensible, as intense mental pressure and constant suppression are equal to a stronger and unpredictable uproar and eruption. Understanding such rapid changes will not be possible for those who suppress, as they have neither the cultural background nor the will to understand the younger generation's world. These can be seen in human relationships. The differences between the new and old generations will also be obvious in various fields, and the contradiction between the political and social perspectives is one of the most fundamental issues.

All these oppressions will generate fear and worry for many previous or traditional generations, as they believe that, due to their higher experience and deeper understanding of society, their thoughts are more realistic and have more foresight than the younger generation who, they claim, are simple-minded, inexperienced, and are unaware that emotions can coexist with rationality. And, yet the existence of emotions in youth is *not* in conflict with rationality.

However, for some conservatives and traditionalists, diversity of beliefs and individuality are not natural and common. They may consider any difference as a deviation and may even fight against it. This lack of understanding of differences and diversity among humans will create a deep cognitive gap, leading to a loss of connection between generations. As history shows, conservative parents or government institutions will never have the ability to process and control the thoughts of the new generation. The information sources that are accessible to the new generation, which feed them intellectually, are so numerous and uncontrollable, and the efforts of religious government supporters and traditional families are practically futile.

Therefore, the level of rule-breaker thoughts and behaviors of Iran's new generation has unexpectedly caused a cultural shock to previous generations. Many of them assumed that they had the power and possibility to control and influence future generations. They thought it would be impossible for their children to think and act differently and oppositely, as the channels of deviation are controlled, and, at the same time, no serious opposition is observed from them, while the current pace of changes in the world and the modern era is incomparable to the times when tradition and religion were alive with such methods in history. The personality of humans is not wholly controllable today, and the mindset of the new generation cannot be processed through outdated tools. The lack of opposition from the new generation in a traditional family or conservative social environment does not mean they're conforming to traditional or religious culture. The level of access to texts or documents that a teenager obtains in a day via technological tools is multiple times more than the content of recommendations and pieces of advice from parents or authorities. Therefore, such methods and paths for the traditional and oppressive systems are undeniable failures.

When Iranian youth do not express their opposition to their families, or social and political systems, in some cases, that has never meant approval or agreement. Opposition and agreement have meaning only in a safe and free environment. Of course, there is a fundamental difference between the Islamic government and traditional parents. The occupying Islamic regime in Iran is a clear example of a terrorist and oppressive regime and has no connection to legitimacy and human rights. Parents, in most cases, unintentionally and benevolently, introduce the imposed culture as an undeniable tradition.

On the other hand, without a doubt, many families have provided a suitable environment for the growth of Generation Z, such as creating a healthy environment for expressing opinions freely and without fear, allowing them to have privacy, and helping to develop their talents and abilities. These are families that have given their children the freedom to think and express opinions freely and consider them an independent part of the family. These are families that have eliminated self-censorship and its origins from the family environment. These are families that have considered privacy for their children so they can experience a sense of individualism and self-attention. These are families that provide comprehensive support to the growth, development, and intellectual maturation of their teenagers and youth. A large part of the new generation of Iranians has been raised in such thoughtful families, families who understand the demands of the current time and have nurtured a questioning and antiauthoritarian generation. These are individuals who do not accept any form of authoritarianism; they cannot imagine that a part of society determines their lifestyle. Rather, they understand and judge, make decisions, and act.

The new generation does not recognize the roles of predecessors and leaders. Creeds of characters and charisma are meaningless for them. Some individuals, during the tragic events of 1357 SH (Islamic Revolution in 1979), were mesmerized by the image of a man named Khomeini on the moon and were influenced insomuch that they shed tears during his speeches for no reason. Such foolishness is unimaginable for today's revolutionary and modern generation. The new generation of Iranians considers those who followed a fraudulent leader blindly to be ignorant, and, as a result, dragged themselves and the country into decline. The new generation is self-reliant and self-motivated, which means they do not have a leader for their revolution. It bravely confronts the most savage and terrorist forces of the government, which does not even hesitate to commit such crimes as killing even children. The best and most liberal Iranians are facing the worst evil and criminals.

The rebellion and intellectual and cultural revolt of Generation Z have paid a significant price for the Islamic regime, as the foundation of the Islamic government is based on the recognition of a supreme leader. The absolute guardianship of the jurist, who has seized all the power in the country, is the fundamental base of the Islamic regime. However, the people of Iran have turned such a pillar into their legitimate target and center of their attacks. This is something maddening for the regime and its supporters. And it shatters all their beliefs and delusions.

If the predecessors of Generation Z had searched for the truth in one person, a group, or a book, or if the leader or guide had the first and final say, then, when he determined which thought or behavior was right or wrong, he gave orders and others obeyed. Then he spoke and others listened. Such a thing in the current situation in Iran is not considered valid and scientific. The new generation of modern Iranians is not unipolar; they are antiauthoritarian, which is why they can rise without a leader. They started protesting and expressing their disgust against the reactionary Mullahs in all parts of Iran in a self-organized manner without a charismatic or specific leader. The binding and gathering tool for them was common concepts and values, not individuals and politicians. Humanistic, democratic, and patriotic values made a resident of Tabriz feel unified and coherent with someone living in Zahedan. Iranians were not united by orders and commands but by focusing on freedom and democracy, which were their common and motivating goals. This combination and consensus at the national level frightened the Islamic government, taking away their power of propaganda and advertising. They even resorted to insulting and belittling official tribunes due to their inability to confront the revolutionary movement of the people.

Ebrahim Raisi, who is the current president of the Islamic regime, had compared the revolutionary people to houseflies in the recitation of a poem, and some of his ministers suggested the Iranian youth go to psychologists for treatment. The form and content of such literature showed the height of failure and inability of the Islamic regime's officials against the Iranian people. They saw everything was lost, and their base of beliefs vanished among the people; as a result, they said inappropriate things to ease their unrest and confusion. Seeing a psychologist and paying attention to mental health can also be a very positive thing, but we can't expect more from the dumb Mullahs of the Islamic regime. The reactionary rulers call the *recourse to psychologists* a measure of human backwardness and use it as a means for a verbal attack. Thus, the occupying Islamic regime, whose thoughts and beliefs have become muddled and unclear, is compelled to resort to derision and use it when their beliefs are being challenged.

On the other hand, the Islamic regime was seeking the leader of this uprising, and, since there was no leader, they did not know whom to attack and which person or group to terrorize. Throughout history, assassinations of party leaders and political movements have always been part of authoritarian political systems, especially the Islamic regime in Iran. The goal would be to eliminate the leaders and destroy any movements. In other words, they would remove the leader and main figures of a group, all of whom relied on the lead person so they could eliminate the entire movement. However, in this revolution, there were no leaders for them to assassinate. They did not know whom to attack or which group or party was responsible for the revolution, and this caused confusion and disorder within the Iranian people's order and their self-motivation.

The new generation courageously, and without a leader, acted so innovatively against the terrorists of the Islamic government in such a way that the terrorists did not know which strategy caused the Iranian uprising to become so strong and precise, nor did they not know toward which symbol to direct their accusations and attacks. When the Islamic government faced such a groundbreaking and extraordinary revolution, it attempted to attribute the people's revolution in Iran to the interventions and engineering of various countries and intelligence organizations of foreign governments. The leader of the Islamic government, Ali Khamenei, who is the symbol of terrorism and wickedness, could not believe such a level of hatred and disgust was directed toward himself. To justify his disgraceful history and ideology, he attributed the Iranian uprising to America and the West by considering the hypotheses of foreign interventions. He tried to undermine the authenticity of the "Woman, Life, Freedom" revolution. However, his outdated and rotten methods were ineffective, as his mental illness and paranoia had no impact on the authenticity and nationality of the

Iranian revolution. On the other hand, as the self-proclaimed ultimate authority of the country, he should be responsible for all events and occurrences, and it is obvious that the revolutionary process and accountability that led him to the trial table both need to be discredited.

It was clear that Khamenei, who was responsible for the crimes of the Islamic regime, would not take responsibility for the consequences of his beliefs and would not respond. He did not believe that his imaginary Islamic palace could collapse this way. He was trying to export the Islamic Revolution out of Iran and, along the way, ignited the Middle East in this path when he suddenly saw that, in the heart of and the perspective of the great nation of Iran, the revolution had reached the edge of destruction. In other words, the reality of Iran contradicted Khamenei's assumptions, and the Iranians made a groundbreaking move that forced him to interpret the external reality and the people's uprising with a banal statement to prevent the collapse of his political and religious identity or to attempt to deny many of the events. The thought process of an ideological and biased person evaluates realities based on unchangeable preconceptions to the level that attempts to minimize a significant event or to ignore a truth. Despite being in an ocean of cognitive errors, he stubbornly believes his beliefs are correct, even if all the evidence and documents do not show that.

RELIGIOUS AUTOCRACY OF UNWORTHY MULLAHS

Both tyrants and dictators (there are slight differences between the two titles) have a strong desire to see and hear something that confirms their beliefs and ideas. If they see something written or hear a speech that is in line with their beliefs, it will be supported and admired. But if it challenges their beliefs, it will make them disgusted and will agitate them. The reason for the dictator's animosity toward the people of Iran is the opposition of the Iranian nation to their thoughts. Iranians have long been a negative factor and the destroyer of all the perceptions and beliefs of the regime's leader and his supporters. They expressed disgust, throughout the revolutionary process, toward him and his poisonous ideology.

The people did not speak of reformist tendencies nor fundamentalist principles, as they knew that both political titles were part of the Islamic Revolution dialogue. The Iranian society knew that all self-proclaimed political parties, such as the reformists or fundamentalists (principlism), used deceptive and moderative methods and acted as good and bad interrogators to guarantee the survival of the Islamic government. The Iranian people did not consider them even worthy of their protests. So instead of that, they attacked the principle of the Guardianship of the Islamic Jurist, the entire structure of the Islamic government, Ali Khamenei as the Supreme Leader, and the totality of the religious system. They attacked the foundation and basis of the Islamic regime comprehensively and decisively. This clear position was a declaration of rejecting the totality of the Islamic government. The "Woman, Life, Freedom" revolution leaves no doubt for domestic and international viewers that the Islamic regime is illegitimate and occupying.

Confronted with such a decisive uprising, the authoritarian Mullah's regime demonstrated its most severe form of suppression by its security forces. The unarmed protesters were confronted with the armed repression of the Islamic regime, but, for every crime the regime committed, a new wave of anger and protests arose.

The main issue is that the methods and models of suppression by the Islamic government are wholly different from most countries because the political Shia ideology and its influence in destabilizing its believers are unique and different. Shia followers have adopted corrupt and wrong models, such as Shah Ismail Safavid and his cannibal soldiers, or they emulate leaders who executed 700 people in a single day while simultaneously raping a captive girl left behind by the tribe leader. They have set corrupt and wrong models that do not consider anything other than hostility, oppression, killing, and rape as criteria for their behavior.

When a religious leader uses the term *absolute* (guardianship of the jurist) for a political position, his crimes also become absolute. Absolute power is dangerous for anyone, even if they have a brilliant history and an acceptable report card. Therefore, having such a position in a political structure that contains religious fundamentalists as its executors is concerning. Hence, absolute political and ideological power, without any inhibitions and restraints, produces terrorists and murderers who attempt to suppress a revolution through chemical attacks and poisoning schools to continue maintaining their power. They satisfy their own delusions and vain ambitions by gambling on the lives of children and teenagers, especially females, of a country, particularly within the heart of educational centers, and they intimidate the people through these avenues. This kind of brutal confrontation with protesting people bewildered and astonished everyone.

How much cruelty and savagery must exist in a political system to attack and poison children and teenagers in schools on a large scale? The Mullahs' hatred and animosity toward Iranian girls and the new and modern generation has no bounds. They commit any crime to prevent opposition and revolution from the Iranian people. Olaf Scholz, the Chancellor of Germany, was shocked at the different and brutal models of confrontation and suppression used by the Mullahs directly firing at and attacking the Iranian people with military equipment.

They ruthlessly and cruelly decimate people so much that it is even more violent and brutal than their response to an invading enemy. The Islamic government used both hot and cold weapons to suppress children, students, and university students on a large scale. The government used tear gas and sonic bombs in elementary schools and among young children to create fear and terror and dissuade people from seeking freedom by displaying their savagery and brutality. They employed such brutal methods to halt the revolution.

By attacking children, the government aimed to declare, *"Children and adults are no different to us, that we do not care about children and teenagers, and that we would ruthlessly target the fighting youth and adults protesting in the streets".*

This method exactly resembled the tactics of the Islamic Caliphate group in Iraq and Syria, known as ISIS. ISIS stated, *"Victory through terror, triumph through intimidation and fear"* as their strategy of war. They produced fear on a large scale to intimidate and break the motivation of opponents and the opposition front.

This method affects some people so much that they halt others from doing things. Parents prevent their children from participating in protests and street battles. Some people are convinced that the structure of the oppressive regime is ruthless and indifferent, and as a result, they stop others. If some people are not courageous enough, by witnessing and hearing such scenes, their conservative behavior overcomes their intention and courage. This method had lost its efficiency because of the unparalleled courage of Iranians as they became more resolute in their anger and stance as a result of witnessing so many crimes. People became more confident and determined in their goals because they kept seeing the endless crimes that had been committed by the Revolutionary Guards, mobilization forces, and police.

The people of Iran were engaged in street-fighting against a regime that knew no limits to their crimes, against a regime that used military equipment and weapons to suppress the people. They fought against armed terrorists and criminals who targeted women, men, and children. If the regime did not have access to firearms and organized weapons in a situation for international reasons, they would have just attacked people with cold weapons and beat them brutally. Many heroes of the Iranian nation, who sacrificed their lives for the people and the path of freedom, were killed by numerous brutal baton blows. The number of casualties is also much more than what was published in the media. For example, just in Zahedan, on 'Bloody Friday', the Islamic regime killed nearly 100 people and injured several hundred others. This number is still terrifying even if it does happen during wars. In one of the hacked bulletins of the Fars News Agency, published by hacker group Black Reward, they announced that the number of casualties in the nationwide protests in Iran was much higher than the deaths of November 2019 (1,500 people) in the Mahshahr massacre.

The Islamic regime did not even spare young children, who were killed, too. They had no limit to their crimes. It is necessary to mention the names of some of the children who were murdered by the terrorists of the Islamic government during the "Woman, Life, Freedom" revolution:

1. Zakaria Khayal, 16 years old, from Piranshahr
2. Amin Marefat, 16 years old, from Oshnavieh
3. Abdullah Mohammadpour, 17 years old, from Baloo Village, Western Azerbaijan
4. Mohammadreza Sarvari, 14 years old, from Tehran
5. Pedram Azarnoush, 16 years old, from Dehdasht, Kohgiluyeh and Boyer-Ahmad
6. Siavash Mahmoudi, 16 years old, from Tehran;
7. Amir Mahdi Farrokhipour, 17 years old, from Tehran
8. Mirhossein Basati, 15 years old, from Kermanshah
9. Nimeh Shafaq Dost, 16 years old, from Urmia

10. Sarina Esmaeilzadeh, 16 years old, from Goldasht Karaj
11. Nika Shakermi, 16 years old, from Tehran
12. Setareh Tajik, 17 years old, from Tehran
13. Mehdi Mosavi Nikoo, 16 years old, from Zanjan
14. Mohammad Amin Gamshadzehi, 17 years old
15. Jabar Shiruzehi, 12 years old
16. Omid Safarzehi, 17 years old
17. Samer Hashemzehi, 16 years old
18. Sadis Kashani, 14 years old
19. Yaser Shahuzehi, 16 years old
20. Mohammad Rokhsani, 12 years old
21. Omid Sarani, 13 years old
22. Ali Barahoui, 14 years old
23. Javad Pusheh, 11 years old
24. Ten people from Zahedan
25. Kian Pirfalak, 9 years old, from Izeh Khuzestan
26. Hasti Naroui, 7 years old, from Zahedan
27. Siavash Mahmoudi, 16 years old, from Tehran

The main question is: In which logic, ideology, and religion is the attack and murder of children justified? Killing children is the biggest evidence and proof of the boundless cruelty of the Islamic regime – a government that represents hostility and kills people easily, a government whose foundation is based on opposition to people's rights and easily kills people who want their basic rights.

If a political system's legitimacy derives from the people, it will have no choice but to obey and accept the people's desires at some point. It is the people who give value and legitimacy to political systems, not the other way around. The occupying Islamic government did not arise from within the people, nor will it be continued by the people. Therefore, they have tried to have the minimum dependency on the people in various fields.

One of the reasons for the ruthless suppression of the Islamic government (besides the savagery of Mullahs' thoughts) is its plan to be only minimally directly dependent on the people. For example, in many countries, the government's financial resources and budgeting depend on people who pay taxes, and if people's taxes are cut off, the system collapses. However, the Islamic government has chosen a different approach and deliberately planned this method. It has become reliant on natural resources, such as oil, gas, and minerals, for its financial independence. Those resources enabled the government to freely carry out any decision it made. In other words, when the required capital is obtained through the sale of crude oil, gas, petrochemical products, and sales of raw minerals, the government will have less direct dependency on the people. The Islamic government knows that the general population is opposed to its foundation and essence and tries to minimize as much as it can its financial dependency so it can preserve its existence in the most vital and urgent conditions and suppress its opponents with greater ease.

The financial independence of political institutions gives more maneuvering power to dictators. The regime's independence from the people also increases its ability to be the winner in an uncontrollable society. So, the Mullahs' alienation from the people and financial independence have strengthened the government's overall sense of dictatorship. It buys military equipment and oppression tools through the sales of land resources and suppresses the nation by training and preparing repressive forces to the utmost extreme. It spends people's wealth against them. It steals the country's natural resources and strengthens itself with the dirty capital, reinforcing the illegitimate foundations of the Islamic government.

Occupying Mullahs, those who neither care about anything related to Iran and Iranians, have not highlighted any of the symbols belonging to Iran and Iranians during their dark rule. The stateless occupying Mullahs and their army (sepah) have a hatred of Iran's name pronounced without ideology. Khamenei and his traitor gangsters have such enmity toward the nation and the history of Iran that they don't even carry Iranian symbols in national ceremonies and celebrations. They censor and remove anything related to their homeland and patriotism.

Where else in the world and on which land has this level of hostility toward national symbols by an established government been witnessed?

Various political systems attempt to forge a false history and create a fake national identity for their countries. They even appropriate famous characters, poets, and writers from other countries by falsifying documents and distorting their names. They care about the importance of their nation and history, and they try excessively to obtain symbols of identity, even with lies. But the Mullahs, deliberately and ideologically, deny the cultural and historical property of the people. They ignore and deny anything related to the nation, nationality, and people to create enough space for implementing their own religious and political ideologies, which have no connection to the people.

Dictators who seek to impose their tyranny usually prioritize personal ambitions and the implementation of party goals. They do not show enmity or hatred toward the country, its resources, and history, but these faceless Mullahs have no feelings or signs of patriotism and friendship toward even their own people. They are just like Khameini, the founder of the Regime in Iran, who confesses to being indifferent and having no emotions about his return to Iran after years of exile.

Islamic government officials in Iran are so alienated from the Iranian people that they speak about the country's issues with disregard and indifference, ignoring the consequences of their disastrous management. However, when they are speaking about their own Islamic militants, they display enthusiasm and excitement. If they talk about Islamic symbols and proxy groups, their delight and zeal are visible in their demeanor and behavior. But speaking about things like the well-being of the people, national interests, and freedom is terrifying and meaningless for them. They are dogmatic and delusional persons who have enslaved a nation with religious and political madness without any basis or principle.

The results and consequences of the behavior of the Islamic regime are the main reasons for the change in the attitude and behavior of the Iranian people. Whatever the Mullahs and the Islamic Revolutionary Guards have said and implemented has turned into backwardness and destruction of the country. Simply put, if the Islamic government has always expressed hostility toward the free world, then the Iranian people have considered friendship with the free world to be the correct position. If the Islamic regime has introduced gender discrimination as a cultural and social value, the Iranian youth have defined gender equality as one of the principles of their revolution. Therefore, Iranians know that whatever the Mullahs consider to be right is actually wrong, and whatever they think to be wrong is right.

This method of conceptualization is also prevalent and understandable in the daily lives of all people on a smaller scale, such as how to recognize negative behavioral traits, like accusation or lying. In other words, persons who lie to their loved ones and try to deceive them will eventually lose their loved ones' trust after a while; others will also reduce or cut off their communication with the liar. The person realizes that lying is a behavioral pattern that results in the loss of relationships, friendships, and social capital. The liar is left alone while their circle of communication (family, friends) becomes limited. Others will likely behave cautiously and not be clear toward the deceiver. This consequence results in the person choosing to act more honestly and truthfully, which are considered to be positive traits. Simply put, if lying leads to the loss of others, then honesty attracts trust. Honesty strengthens and deepens the link between individuals. Therefore, understanding correct behavior and position through the experience of the consequences of incorrect actions can also be among the methods of increasing political understanding on a larger scale. That is why reversing the thoughts and goals of the Mullahs and government institutions can illuminate the correct and appropriate path.

The Iranian people have experienced laws and objectives outlined in the constitution and structure of the Islamic regime, which have led to severely harmful consequences for the citizens and the future of Iran.

The Islamic regime has hindered development and progress and dragged all the possessions and lives of the citizens toward ruin and destruction. In such an accelerated trend toward absolute darkness, opposing the beliefs and objectives of the ruling powers, Mullahs, and the Islamic revolutionary guards would be the most suitable option for the people.

From the incorrect thoughts and positions of Mullahs, one can identify the correct position. The Iranian society has been living under the management style of the Mullahs not for a few months or years, but for several decades, all the while not being willing to accept such a governance model and imposed suffocation. Iranians live in a country with the most natural resources, the world's largest reserves of oil and gas, plus it's a rich and historic country. So why do they have the weakest economic situation and experience the most regrettable conditions, in terms of welfare and freedom? This tragic catastrophe has occurred due to the existence of corrupt and unworthy leaders and a kleptocratic and inefficient political and management structure.

After all, the Iranian people, who have been living in a society with wrong structures and religious orientations, have not lost hope for achieving freedom and democracy. They have firmly said, *"NO!"* to the totalitarian Islamic government's propaganda. Iranians demand the replacement of absolute despotism with secular democracy, Islamic values with liberal values, gender discrimination with gender equality, censorship with transparency, and closed doors based on ideology with open doors based on national interests. Such rationality and tendencies have worried the Islamic government because the sale of religion and ideology has not yielded any results and has failed among the Iranian people in the public sphere.

All the Islamic government's efforts have been to justify and legitimize the Mullahs' rule by using religious content and beliefs while other people reject such a notion in their revolutionary uprising. On the other hand, considering the process of the "Women, Life, Freedom", revolution, the officials of the Islamic regime, in addition to observing the defeat and fragmentation of their own ideology, saw their positions and government support at risk. Accountability is difficult and intolerable for those who are not accustomed to being accountable. It is clear that, in such a situation, the Mullahs and the terrorist institution of the Islamic Revolutionary Guards consider the protesting people as a threat. 'Money is more valuable than blood' for them. And they use any method to weaken the Iranian people's demand for freedom. They must give up all their government positions in a democratic structure and become accountable for all their behaviors. They are not willing to give up such lucrative and influential positions by standing behind the trial bench. They consent to murdering the Iranian people, including even children. In this situation, the people are allowed to use any method and way they find useful to overthrow the structure of the Islamic regime.

RADICAL BELIEVERS AND ALIENATED MERCENARIES

Repressive and security forces of the Islamic regime (Guardians of the Islamic Revolution, mobilization forces, riot police, intelligence agencies, and security forces) that engage in violence and suppression against Iranian freedom and democracy activists fall into two groups and categories:

- They are either mean mercenaries who are willing to commit crimes for immediate benefit gain, or
- They are delusional extremists who, through brainwashing and their religious beliefs, consider crimes against humanity to be a good and right thing.

Of course, both parts of this division fall under psychological disorders, and disorders can be analyzed and treated psychologically. How have the environmental conditions and the growth situation of such individuals have been? How were their childhoods and teen years? Which are the most serious periods of growth and personality formation? And how much did they experience positive and negative things? How much did genetics and background factors affect them? To what extent have other factors, such as poverty, deprivation, and humiliation, played a role in the emergence of such individuals? And to what extent did the structure and anatomy of the brains of these individuals have problems and dysfunction? All these factors can contribute to the committing of crimes by a person.

Naturally, human behavior is not affected by a single cause and it is not unidimensional. However, various factors contribute to the occurrence of a behavior. The matter in this section is the final and determining factor of the occurrence of crimes by the thugs and hooligans of the Islamic regime, the factor that is the direct cause of all possible same characteristics. The ideology plays a significant role for believers who have the delusion of truth in their minds, and, in contrast, money and financial interests are essential elements for mercenaries and opportunists.

Mercenaries are individuals who commit acts without the belief in or any regard for humanity, ethics, laws, and rights to receive a specific payment. Some individuals engage in anything in exchange for money. They murder, harass, threaten, and damage others' property, easily violate others' rights, close their eyes to all principles and values, and do not care about such behavior. They will, without hesitation, use any means and behavior necessary that leads to more money and a higher income, even if it harms their families and friends. They bring their nation and homeland to the brink of weakness and destruction and compromise the freedom, democracy, and security of the people with money.

This kind of thing not only happens in dictatorships but also in the most democratic countries; some individuals disregard everything and everyone for their own financial goals. All these instances fall under the concept of mercenary, whether they are stone-age Mullahs holding guns or politicians wearing ties and smiling. Such behavior substantially contradicts the culture that sacrifices everything for the sake of humanity because the main priority for a mercenary is money and personal interests, not humanity. However, noble humans place humanity at the center of all matters, like the statue of honor of Iranian Dr. Aida Rostami, who secretly went from house to house during the "Woman, Life, Freedom" revolution to provide medical care to those wounded in the fight against the Islamic regime, until the Islamic regime's agents discovered her covert medical activities so they kidnapped, tortured, and killed her. She sacrificed her position, status, and resources and risked her life while fulfilling medical and humanitarian missions. The difference between human-like mercenaries and noble humans is indescribable.

The matter of mercenary has changed from a partial and personal state in the modern world into what is now an industry that operates such jobs in an organized manner. Such organizations include armies and private military companies.

The job of such companies is to participate in proxy or direct wars in exchange for receiving money from governments. They are given large sums of money through this process at the cost of human lives. They engage in conflicts and armed clashes, and they advance the war in a way that achieves the objectives of their client countries. It is not important to them if they have the right or not to do their job or if their front is true or false on the battlefield. Money and financial contracts are what motivates them to do their shady actions and military intervention.

An example of one such private company is The Wagner Group, a Russian mercenary group that has carried out military operations on behalf of Russia. This group essentially does not care about how Russia's policies are determined, or whether they are in the interest of even the Russian people, or against Russian national interests. Also, the group pays no mind to if the people they are up against are violators or supporters of human rights. For them, the quantity and quality of the contract dollar amount determines how they behave. If Russia openly commits military aggression against an independent country, like Ukraine, and attempts to occupy it, companies like Wagner are suitable options for intervention.

In exchange for securing contracts and receiving large sums of money, the administrators of such companies send their forces and mercenaries to areas under occupation to massacre Ukrainian citizens. By showing a more brutal face than the Russian army, they create more terror and fear.

They are not and have never been committed to the international rules of war and human rights (international laws of armed conflict). Individuals and forces fighting in this group and similar companies are mercenaries. In other words, they have chosen crime and villainy as their profession without considering who the opposing party (or parties) is and the reason why they are being murdered.

These mercenaries have considered offense and crime as a job, regardless of who the opponent is and the reason they are being killed. They make the world ugly and unbearable. They are called mercenaries because they care only about throwing a bone in exchange for their services to set the gears of the killing machine in motion. To put it simply, they are thugs who are organized at various levels, from local to international, and carry out their atrocities in a more organized and structured manner.

With this explanation, many individuals who have played a role in the suppression and massacre of the Iranian people now fall under the concept of the mercenary. They oppress and kill regardless of the people they face, driven by the accolades and money they receive. They kill, injure, torture, and humiliate Iranian individuals because they will not commit to any identity characteristic, moral values, or even national and patriotic values that the Islamic regime forces on them! The mercenaries do not even believe in the values of the company they are working for. There is no difference – to them – between the Islamic Revolutionary Guard Corps, the army, the police forces, or any other group or organization. It doesn't matter if they even work in companies or organizations that are against the Islamic regime. The determining factor for them in choosing their war front is the amount of money each side offers. The values of that system are not important to them. Whether the goal is to spread Islamic Shia religion, Sunni religion, promote Communism, or liberalism, it doesn't make any difference to mercenaries. They will fight for every and any goal and ideal because their aim does not depend upon such matters. What they *do* depend on is any set of goals or ideals that increases their income and guarantees their financial security, just as the American newspaper *The Washington Post* reported, based on information from U.S. security agencies, that Yevgeny Prigozhin, the commander of The Wagner Group, had offered to sell information about the positions of the Russian army forces to Ukraine.

The second sector of the repressive forces is the villainous delusional persons, who have religious faith and ideological opinions and attempt to suppress, kill, and torture. These oppressors have goals and ideals. Unlike the mercenaries, to whom principles and values are worthless, these villainous delusional people believe that the Islamic government is a sacred political system that gets its legitimacy from God and religion, not from the people. Its legitimacy comes from the divine rules, and the legitimate roots of the Islamic regime are in heaven, and not in this earthly realm. According to them, people have no right to oppose such a government in any way. The fourth law of the regime's constitution refers to this matter, and it is the reason why the leader of the Islamic regime, Ali Khamenei, has this perspective.

In the middle of suppressing the Iranians' uprising, comparing the regime to an unshakeable tree, he said, *"That seedling is a mighty tree, and no one should dare think they can uproot it."* In other words, from the point of view of the Mullahs, people have no right to overthrow the government and that people have no right to determine their own destiny and execute their political will.

When political and governance legitimacy comes from God, people naturally do not have the right to change it. Citizen satisfaction and political acceptability are irrelevant to them.

Mesbah Yazdi, one of the theorists of Islamic governance, always said, *"Do people have such a right to grant?"* These people do not recognize the right to enforce the law and governance of the people, so the nation does not have the right to change the political system. The Islamic regime has instilled such a belief among some simple-minded believers and created the notion that Islamic governance is a government that inherits the mission and message from divine prophets. Mullahs consider themselves the heirs of so-called prophets. They claim that, if any weakness arises in the Islamic governance or if such a government were to be destroyed, then all the efforts and struggles of divine prophets will be in vain. And, if the political system is not based on religion and the Mullahs' beliefs, then the foundation of religion will be lost.

Over time, this belief system gets stronger for some believers, and they consider the protection of such a government to be a religious duty. They imagine that if they are killed while protecting such a system, God will be pleased with them. If they suppress the regime's opponents and become guardians of the regime, they will be considered among the warriors of God. They believe they are on the truth side, and as a result, they become engaged in suppressing individuals who are on the side of falsehood. They consider Islam and the Islamic government as absolute truth and anyone opposing it is foreign and an enemy. They consider the fighting and suppression of the people of Iran to be silencing evildoers and enemies of God and regard them as enemies of God or militants.

For a human to have that kind of behavior and to carry out such atrocities against other humans takes a person with a very strong, unwavering faith, albeit the opposite of rational thinking. This faith allows any evil behavior to be justified in the minds of its believers. Ideology and deep faith create madness that leaves no space for doubt in actions. They become killers without remorse. They torture with satisfaction. They blind with a smile and assault with no hesitation.

It is logical that, as the level of responsibility and influence of someone's behavior increases, their goals must be more justified and certain as well. With this view, since attacking citizens and compatriots is the most heinous act possible, the oppressor clings to the necessity of this action by justification. They introduce a backing of God, divine scriptures, and religious leaders as justifications for their behavior. And, to top it all off, they believe they do *not* have responsibility for their actions. To escape responsibility and hide behind a justification, the concept of God and an abstract religion are the most elusive and inaccessible. If they commit a crime, it will be in line with the goals of religion and strengthening the religious system. They justify their violent behavior toward society with divine approval and support for their religion. They rationalize the responsibility for killing people in their minds through ideological beliefs.

Some of the oppression forces of the Islamic government in Iran use such religious faith and easily commit murders of citizens. The Islamic government has planned the creation of such oppressive and faithful forces since the childhood and adolescence of Iranians, as such monsters will not emerge in a short time. The production and propagation of such forces require a lengthy process of deepening their faith and belief.

Mullahs have tried to corrupt the minds of people from various paths, including the media, art, schools, mosques, and even universities, to protect the power and position that have so easily achieved. It is a position that they never anticipated having, not even in their dreams. In other words, those who were unable to do anything other than recite prayers at the graves of the deceased and always living by the labor of other people, when they gained political power, used any opportunity in every possible way to continue chasing political activists in Iran and not sparing anything from murder, killings, imprisonment, or torture. The Mullahs know that losing power is equal to being held accountable and being tried for the responsibilities they had, which would entail a return to their previous hypocritical life with tattered clothes, and losing the money and possessions they have looted. Therefore, they need a repressive machine and necessary human resources to carry out the murders. They need faithful persons who protect the Mullahs and their wealth while completely giving up their own thoughts and ideas and continuing willingly to stay in captivity. They are ready to commit any crime against their compatriots, and due to religious faith and other underlying reasons, they do not feel remorse. Mullahs need repressive forces who believe that killing and suppressing people and opposing freedom is supporting religion and God and that this is their religious duty. Mullahs are merchants who sell abstract concepts (God, religion, the afterlife) to a group of people but make the delivery of the goods conditional on life after death. They are merchants who have transformed the real and tangible world into hell and exchanged their goods in the form of credit.

If the faithful oppressors are asked why they kill their own countrymen and what goal and justification they have for doing that, their answer is: *"It is to support the divine Islamic system and to strengthen God's religion!"*

But, in reality, how does supporting God and religion lead to the consolidation of which person and in which position? Whose power is strengthened? The answer is neither God nor religion. God is not among humans on Earth and does not have a physical presence, rather, it is a representative claiming to exist on Earth. Since God is not physically present to govern, and on the other hand, religion is based on faith, therefore, in society, supporting God and religion means to support the representative of God and the executor of religion. Who will this representative and executor be? Well, one Mullahs will introduce themselves as the representative of God, prophets, and the executor of religious commandments. With this explanation, assisting the religion of God through oppressive powers will result in nothing but direct support and assistance for the stability of the Mullahs' position and the survival of despotism.

The Mullahs and guards who have infiltrated all aspects of governance in the country have considered such a matter through staggering budgets to reproduce such simple-minded believers to protect them in times of upheaval with all their strength. Even the policy of increasing the population did not have any goal other than providing human resources (militants, mobilization forces, and suppressors), and the aging of the Iranian population, was just an excuse to propagate the next generations to achieve the human force resources, which is needed by the regime's ideology. For the Mullahs, the future and interests of the people, youth, and children are meaningless. For religious fundamentalists, the oppressed people of Sistan and Baluchestan are not important. They have abandoned them in a way that they do not have enough food and drink, are deprived of basic education, and even a large part of the population doesn't have identification documents. The aging process of the Iranian population and taking into account the interests of the Iranian nation is meaningless for them. They consider the current living conditions of youths and children, engulfed in an ocean of problems, to be worthless and insignificant. Do the Mullahs who, like thieves, gave the stolen capital and wealth belonging to the oppressed Baluch, Kurd, and Azerbaijani children to terrorists, like Hassan Nasrallah, the leader of Hezbollah in Lebanon, feel any sense of humanism or patriotism at all?

Humans are like hardware, and religious ideology is like software. Therefore, population increase and ideology promotion will further increase the chances of survival and consolidation of power for the Mullahs and support such a regime. They promote procreation and make population growth one of the main goals of the regime and part of their overall policies. Mullahs do not consider life, freedom, and welfare to be desirable for humans, nor do they want it. They do not plan and set goals for it. Instead, they aim to produce obedient followers and create a herd of militants. Their ultimate goal is to have a large population with endless problems and a larger number of obedient citizens. If there is no positive vision for the future of people and proportional welfare, it doesn't matter. As long as they are alive and obedient to the regime's malicious goals, that is enough for the Mullahs.

With this description, we can better identify the reason for the high level of religious propaganda and the reason why religious institutions produce toxic intellectual food in various forms for children and adolescents. Dictators know that children are less likely to demand reasons from the claimant to accept ideas and beliefs, and they accept words and claims easily without feeling the need for justifiable reasons, due to their young age.

Due to the influence of the environment and the dominance of emotions, many of them tend to think and contemplate which is why children are considered to be an easy target for the government system. Children can easily be molded into desired shapes (figuratively, of course). For this reason, parents must pay strong attention to, and be vigilant to, prevent their children from falling into the trap of the manipulative and deceitful practices of the Islamic regime for such a system poses a threat to the lives and futures of so many Iranian children – this early negative impact on children's minds will be evident in family relationships.

The Mullahs see today's young children as the suppressors of the future and create psychotic and deviant personalities in them. In the context of ideologies, especially religious ones, there is a factor present that can turn a person into someone who can commit criminal acts without remorse or the slightest discomfort. The existence of belief and confidence in the righteousness and correctness of one's actions aligned with his or her faith is one of the main drivers of people committing crimes without feeling guilty. In other words, self-confidence and self-righteousness in carrying out oppression and massacre are based on a strong faith in the Mullah's ideology.

Racists and racial supremacists do not attack others from a position of weakness or a sense of inferiority but rather from a position that shows the self-righteousness that they firmly believe in. They believe that their race is superior and better than others (even though there is no biological basis for racial concepts in the Islamic regime). This self-perceived superiority gives them the audacity to easily carry out brutal actions, such as imprisonment, elimination, and physical attacks. This same mindset has led the regime's oppressive forces, with their self-confidence derived from faith and a strong belief in the superiority of Muslims over others, to take up arms and justify their atrocities with a calm conscience against protesters and revolutionaries.

By polarizing society and creating social divisions, the government has caused a gap within the community. Drawing a line between good and evil among citizens justifies oppressing a large portion of the population, labeling them as the evil side. A prerequisite for this false confidence and self-righteousness is the polarization of the ideological environment in society. Polarizing society and introducing one side as right and the other as wrong creates a division among people and leads some to believe that they have all the rights and their opponents have none. However, the foundation of democracy lies in accepting pluralism and involving individuals in equal participation, which helps to prevent the emergence of such divisions. When there is no equality in the law but equality against the law, and some individuals enjoy special privileges based on such factors as gender, religion, or allegiance to the government, while others are considered second-class or third-class citizens, it will pave the way for social fragmentation.

For example, on the issue of freedom concerning clothing in Iran, the deprived and powerless members of society were denied the right to dress freely while certain other groups, under the pretext of religion, enjoyed the privileges of the ruling authority's power and could freely choose their own attire. In other words, they were allowed to choose their clothing according to their taste, while others were not. They would appear in public places, indoors and outdoors, wearing clothes that demonstrate their adherence to religious laws and the Islamic government. However, if one of the deprived and powerless citizens wants to dress according to their preferences and desires, it is prohibited and condemned. These two dichotomies – the privileged and deprived – pitted against each other could lead to social collapse.

The government considers obedient and loyal individuals to be citizens. It labels those who do not believe in the Islamic system of governance and structure as second-class citizens or even villains and enemies of the nation. With their increasing quantity and quality, these kinds of divisions will pit fellow citizens (revolutionaries and suppressors) against each other, resulting in no positive feelings toward each other, ultimately demonstrating such false divisions on the streets as offensive and defender or revolutionary and suppressor. Due to government support and regime propaganda, some will consider themselves to be the absolute truth and their fellow citizens who stand against the regime to be absolute evil. With this unrealistic perception, those who are suppressive and self-righteous would be glad to confront the people.

This is how illegitimate systems spread seeds of division and cause conflicts within society. In critical moments, they allow believers and supporters to eliminate their fellow citizens to preserve their power. Religious propagators also use various possible methods to instill, in military forces, the belief that suppressing and committing violence against people is sacred and divine, such as using religious stories from the scriptures, the martyrdom of Imam Hussein, wars, and the behavioral traditions of the Islamic prophet against disbelievers, as well as the governance of the first Imam of Shia and his descendants. It is within this process that the "Woman, Life, Freedom" revolution has lost many martyrs, heroes, victims, and those subjected to torture, while the suppressive faction sees itself as faithful and considers suppressing society as sacred and jihad, imagining their all-encompassing violent actions as being in the right position.

THE RIGHT OF FUNDAMENTAL CHANGE

Governments exist for *the implementation of the will of the citizens, welfare, and people's security*. The establishment of a government and its survival should also be supported by the people and achieve maximum acceptance. Such popular approval must be consciously and freely developed in a healthy democratic environment. Electoral games and theatrical and political activities with ballot boxes have no relevance to democracy in authoritarian countries.

Elections are intended to reflect the views of the people and make changes. In systems where parties and individuals do not change, the ballot box becomes meaningless and futile, just like the word Republic that the Islamic regime is trying to carry – a meaningless and unrelated term for the political regime in Iran. In any country where people aren't able to express their opinions through elections and peaceful methods, all populist titles will be false and fabricated.

Mullahs refer to their regime as a republic, but they have prohibited any structural changes and suppressed the activities of various parties. Therefore, there is no way for people to express their opinions on how the country should be managed. The Mullahs have imposed a model of governance on the people by force and coercion while blocking peaceful paths for change. Only one party is allowed to operate; it is the one that supports and represents the Islamic government. Claims that parties, like reformists, fundamentalists, or conservatives, exist are more like satire than political reality.

All parties within the discourse of the Islamic revolution have followed a common goal and motivation. They have sought and continued to strengthen the Islamic government system in various situations through populist techniques.

All of them believe in the guardianship of the jurist, political Islam, resistive economy, and enmity toward the West and

America. The Islamic regime wholly eliminated and destroyed partisan politics, and the people of Iran have not been deceived by the regime's old methods and party games. It is remarkable that in the "Women, Life, Freedom" revolution, people did not chant slogans even against various fake parties. They considered them ineffective and against their own movement for freedom. Iranians are aware of the issue that there is no difference between the so-called Islamic parties because they all have specific goals and ideological beliefs. Many of them resort to weapons and use violence as a tool to counter democracy whenever the principle of the Islamic regime is threatened.

Sadegh Zibakalam, who is a professor of political science at the University of Tehran, always falsely presents himself as a liberal, as he had stated in a well-known interview:

"Ms. Shahrabi, I would take one step further and be very clear and explicit, without playing with words so that I can later say that was not my intention. Ms. Shahrabi played tricks, and I don't know if she manipulated this part of the interview and these... No... Ms. Shahrabi, you see what I'm trying to say, I'm trying to be very simple and explicit, so that I can't escape from it later. If things come to a point where people rise up against the principles of the Islamic system, with this Guardian Council and the supervisory powers, with this Islamic Consultative Assembly and the esteemed leader, I, Sadegh Zibakalam, will take up weapons and fight against the people and prevent the downfall."

Such dishonest university professors, who introduce themselves as intellectuals, have become outdated and discredited with the advent of the modern Iranian revolution and have been disarmed through the Iranian youth revolution.

In a suppressive situation where people are wholly disappointed with the change and transformation in the country's management system and cannot find any openings or ways to express their opinions freely, it is obvious that they will not see any way to change anything other than a revolution ahead of them. They consider themselves hostages of a few individuals who have played with the fates of the country's citizens with their empty ideologies. The Mullahs steal and loot the country's natural resources, capital, and people's wealth, and openly spend it for their own interests and the promotion of Islamic ideology. The people never wanted such a situation. The fundamental rule is that the people of any country should be the ones to make decisions regarding national wealth and its distribution methods. They are the ones who introduce and endorse political representatives and agents in terms of international relations and the manner of governing the country. Otherwise, none of the regime's positions and decisions will not be credible. The question is: Who introduced (and how) the Islamic regime as the representative of the Iranian people? How did they implement any plan or program without people's consent or without declaring their views?

The behavior of the Islamic government in the Middle East and the regime's direct and indirect interventions in the collapse or continuation of oppressive governments were never and will not be approved by the Iranian people. The prominent characteristic of the Iranian people is the desire for freedom and democracy, but the regime seeks to stabilize and support dictatorships. Therefore, the actions of the Islamic regime in the region and the world have no connection to the desires and will of the Iranians. Weakening and destroying democracies is part of the Islamic government's agenda, which includes countries from Lebanon and Syria to Venezuela, a country that suffers at the hands of a lunatic named Nicolas Maduro. From North Korea and the fascist regime of China to European separatist groups and many anti-democracy leftists in America, they have solid relations with the Mullahs' regime.

In return, the Mullahs have created dark and murky relations with all democracies. They consider the European Union and the free world to be their enemies, labeling Western and liberal lifestyles as contagious viruses. Any government or nation that speaks out about human rights and freedom angers the Mullahs. Intellectuals and academics who support suppression and suffocation and simultaneously show hostility toward America and the free world are warmly welcomed by the Mullahs, regardless of whether they are leftists or fascists, like Alexander Dugin. They have even reached such audacity that they openly support oppressive regimes worldwide. Even at a time when all countries around the world have condemned the Russian invaders in Ukraine and the criminal Vladimir Putin, they shamelessly and openly declared support and sacrifice for the aggression. The self-proclaimed leader of Islamists, Ali Khamenei, has openly and explicitly supported Russia's invasion of Ukraine. The Chinese Communist Party, which is considered the most dangerous threat to democracy in the world, did not even dare to do such a thing!

Although Russia and China have the closest possible relations, the Chinese government takes a controlled and conservative position regarding Russia's military aggression in Ukraine.

The government of Xi Jinping, with its Communist ideology tendencies that have brought dictatorship to a new level in the world (digital dictatorship), a system that is cruel and oppressive, not only didn't dare militarily support Russia's invasion but also did not provide explicit diplomatic support. However, the Mullahs' ignorance and madness policy openly supports the invasion it's fabricating excuses for – Russia's aggression – and provides military support and has supplied Russia with a wide range of military weapons and attack drones. The Mullahs knew that the invading Russians, the Wagner mercenaries, and the Chechen could not confront the brave and patriotic Ukrainians. Therefore, they proceeded to supply the necessary military weapons to Russia. The Islamic Republic regime and its Ayatollahs have provided an amount of support to Russia in its invasion of Ukraine that no other country or government in the world could. This blatant and obvious evidence shows that the most ignorant and brutal persons have taken control of the government in Iran. These positions (which the Islamic regime is taking) have no connection to the desires of the Iranian people and do not represent the opinions of Iranians.

Islamic fundamentalists, who spare no crime to suppress and massacre their own people, are clearly not concerned about the people of Ukraine or other nations.

Such governments will not commit any change in the political system. In developed and democratic countries, ways for changing the system and government are defined and specified. If people are dissatisfied with how the country is running, they can follow peaceful and legal paths and create a smooth ground for parties and individuals to rise to power. Democracies have learned from historical experiences that just a country's citizens should determine the model of governance. Of course, to implement the desires and will of the people, it is necessary to know their opinions. As long as it is not clear which direction the will of the people is headed, it is also impossible to execute it. Therefore, democratic political systems take into account a structure and process to identify the will and desires of the people, allowing citizens to freely and transparently express their wishes.

Components such as freedom of parties, free flow of information, civil institutions, unrestricted journalist activities, accurate voting systems, freedom of speech, freedom of assembly and protests, and an independent judiciary are some of the main elements of a democratic structure, along with recognition of the will and opinions of the people. If a government uses elections to show democracy without implementing the necessary characteristics and components, not only is it *not* democracy but is also a deceitful dictatorship. In other words, it is both the acts of tyranny and deception. A system that uses such methods is neither rooted in the people's will nor legitimated. Rather, it is a dictatorial system that, in the 21st century, is somewhat cautious about expressing its absolute tyranny to international communities and the global society.

Since the concept of democracy and reflecting the will of the people is among the accepted principles of the international and global governing system, some are pursuing tyranny with the façade of democracy, which is not even minority democracy. It is a dictatorship. The main and fundamental feature of democracies is the power of the people to remove the government and replace it with their desired system. Impeachment and removal of a political figure is a more important feature than the installation and establishment of that figure. It is of special importance that the people can easily remove the political system and politicians through defined ways if they are dissatisfied. Because a government is representative of the people who reside in the country, and if the nation does not want such representation, the path of change and ability to overthrow the government should be defined and clear.

The rational and logical paths of change determined in democracies are the results of collective wisdom and lived experience. With the proper foresight, there will be no need for revolution, conflict, or war between the government and the people. The existence of such a model of governance has been to protect the lives, the property, and the valuable opinions of the people. Considering this fact, what kind of reaction is appropriate and logical when governments seize power and block ways of change? If people are opposed to the established government and wish to remove the structure and replace it with another model, and if a dictator has eliminated the paths of change and resorted to suppressing the people at the same time, which remaining method would be more pragmatic and reasonable in such a situation?

This question has no answer except for revolution. This image is exactly what happened in Iran. The revolution of "Woman, Life, Freedom" is faced with such a situation. The Islamic government has occupied political power under the slogans of welfare and respecting people's rights, but, for the past 44 years, it has been trying to control Iranians through various suppressive and suffocating methods. The Iranian people have also tried to change and replace the system, laws, and structure using every possible method, but they have always faced Mullahs' widespread suppression. In one example, according to an exclusive report by the Reuters news agency, during the November 2019 uprising, the Islamic regime's leader ordered the protests to be ended "by any means necessary". So, 1,500 people were killed by the Islamic government. This number is not for injuries; it is the number of deaths. It is a number that is terrifying even if it happens in classic or official wars. It is impossible for a government that kills, imprisons, and tortures its citizens and youth to allow a change in the system through democratic and civil ways.

The people of Iran are inevitably in need of a revolution, literally, and it is obvious that the Islamic government will employ the widest range of suppression and violence against the people. The real battle between the nation and the regime will be the determining factor. If, in the past, there were no instruments of mass communication and everything was done secretly and clandestinely, some people tried to suspiciously link the Islamic government's violence to another issue or hide the role of the crimes committed by the Mullahs and the Islamic Revolutionary Guard's terrorist institution by emphasizing another actor (enemies, hypocrites, security disruptors, spies). However, the existence of technological tools helped people to display the level of cruelty and savagery of the regime and disgraced this deceitful group.

Nevertheless, the Iranian people are capable of overthrowing the Islamic regime in any possible way. In fact, by confronting a terrorist Mullah who seeks to suppress the people in any possible way, the people also have the right to eliminate and remove them in any possible way. The Iranian society has started a revolutionary path that is truly progressive and avant-garde. It is a revolution that is not of the backward and ideological revolutions, but rather, a secular, modern, and liberal uprising. Iranians demand the removal of the Islamic government and its replacement with a secular democracy based on human rights and on a political system that is centered on human rights rather than individuals or religions. Some people who hold governmental positions in different countries misinterpret and misrepresent the desires and goals of the Iranian nation. Such an act is clearly a betrayal of the efforts of a nation seeking freedom. As an example, an American diplomat, named Robert Malley, expressed that the goal of the revolution was that people were seeking respect from the Iranian government. Disregarding the fact that the Islamic regime fundamentally is not legitimated to either grant or withhold respect, the people do not demand reforms or respect. The people of Iran do not desire partial or reformist demands from the ruling authority. Iranians reject the whole foundation of the Islamic regime and seek the removal of the Islamic government.

If some diplomats are pursuing their own interests and signing oil and gas contracts or agreements in the nuclear field with the Islamic government, distorting the Iranian people's intentions firstly, they are undoubtedly traitors to humanity and secondly, traitors to the values of liberalism. If the West is facing energy supply problems despite the war between Russia and Ukraine and is looking for alternative ways, every false action can't be justified, legitimated, or diverted to achieve that goal. Reducing the Iranian people's revolution goal against the Islamic regime to a request for respect is a lie and conservative approach to speak on behalf of the people and create an opportunity for the Islamic government to sign contracts in the energy and nuclear fields, simultaneously.

If America had been introduced as a symbol of democracy, they have been the achievements of freedom fighters, such as Thomas Jefferson, Benjamin Franklin, and George Washington. The principles and values of liberalism and attention to human freedom have created value for the United States. If some opportunist politicians try to profit at any cost by abusing democracy, they will have betrayed the fundamental principles and rules of their own country (although there is a weakness and problem in the capitalist system and its symbol and emblem, America, this defect does not have any connection to the positions of Communists and Socialists; they are fighting in their own world with abundant wealth that nourishes with blood and money).

If interests and unrestrained profiteering are justified, then Chinese politicians are more skilled and adept than Western politicians. The difference in principles and foundations of a system from another system becomes visible not only in slogans but also in behaviors and sensitive conditions. A country that considers human rights as the forefront of its values should fully support the revolution and democrats if it gets caught up in a contradiction between the 'oil and nuclear agreement or supporting the Iranian revolution.' If it fails to make such a choice and tries to reduce or ignore the people's uprising, this is no different from a Chinese politician supporting despotism.

Of course, it is clear that the Iranian people's revolution garnered lots of support from countries, and many American and European politicians sponsored Iranian people. A black-and-white analysis of these subjects may engage us in bias and fallacy. Useful and influential support has also been provided by countries, parties, and politicians. For example, the Article 15 and 25-Point plans, proposed by the German parliament, were in support of the Iranian people's revolution, and the feministic and women-centered foreign policy of German Minister of Foreign Affairs, Annalena Baerbock, was about positive and influential activities and considered to be a positive action. Expelling the Islamic regime from the United Nations Commission on the Status of Women, proposed by the United States to the commission, was also considered to be a positive behavior.

It may be answered that countries develop their policies and behaviors based on the pursuit of national interests. In this case, Iranians' hope for other countries to act is not logical and realistic. This is true, but not completely, therefore it has flaws because national interests are not absolute and unlimited. National interests are limited to certain frameworks. Governments have the right to secure their interests within the framework of international laws. For example, governments are not allowed to commit genocide and colonization in another territory under the pretext of securing national interests. A political system is not allowed to compromise the fundamental rights of humans in exchange for self-interest, profit, or national interests.

This limitation will be even more significant for democratic countries with humanistic rules, as governments that do not prioritize human values are restricted only by the framework of international laws and may even violate these laws if they have the opportunity. In fact, international laws have tried to prevent governments, like the Communist regime in China and the Islamic regime, from spreading wickedness and chaos.

However, governments that consider human values and rights as their fundamental criteria have also defined the second limitation within the framework of fundamental and human values. As a result, they cannot justify any position, decision, or action with the phrase national interests. Such governments are obligated to act in line with national interests when considering these two conditions:

1. they do not violate international laws; and
2. they do not violate human rights.

For example, one of the countries that displayed highly improper behavior during the process of the "Woman, Life, Freedom" revolution was the Swiss government. The behavior of the Swiss government damaged the reputation and position of Switzerland as a country and left a dark memory of it. When the European Union imposed sanctions against the regime and officials of the Islamic government in two cases, due to their behavior (massacre of the Iranian people and military aid and delivery of drones and weapons to Russia), the Swiss government did not join those sanctions. In its declaration, the Swiss government's excuse was quite similar to the Russian and Chinese governments' deceptive statements and excuses. The reason for the declaration was this: Internal and external interests of Switzerland prevent the enforcement of sanctions against the Islamic government. This general statement was the reason the Swiss government gave for turning a blind eye to the massacre and torture of Iranians.

The point is that these sanctions were divided into two parts. The first part was about suppressing the Iranian people, and the second part was about the military intervention of the Islamic regime in the war against Ukraine. The Swiss government agreed and supported the sanctions in the second part but not the first part, which was related to the massacre and suppression of the Iranian people. This behavior was the most disgusting unimaginable political behavior from the political system of Switzerland, a country that has always claimed to be committed to human rights, peace, and humanism. To what extent can it act contradictory?

This dual behavior means that human rights fundamentally do not matter in the face of our greater financial interests and monetary benefits. The banking industry, which is the backbone of the Swiss economic system, remains filled with deposits from officials of the Islamic government while financial and banking transactions continue. These are the same people whose stolen money is kept in various forms in the banks of Zurich, Bern, and Basel. But we close our eyes to the massacre and suppression of humans.

Sanctioning the Islamic regime will certainly prevent the accumulation of such ill-gotten wealth in a mountainous country like Switzerland, which lacks natural resources. Human rights should be a slogan for beyond borders, but our own home should be beautiful and peaceful, with flowing rivers and green trees, and our people should be prosperous. It does not matter if, in the homes of other people, there is fire, smoke, and blood. The notable point here is that when it comes to Russia's aggression toward Ukraine, the situation becomes different. The Swiss government feels a danger lying in wait. They do not impose even minimal sanctions on the Iranian regime for using weapons against children. But they imposed sanctions on the same regime for delivering weapons to a lunatic who might one day threaten their own country or want to go to the Alps. Although the people of Iran and Ukraine both fought against the invasion and demonstrated against the aggressors in various protests and gatherings, the Swiss government shows discrimination among nations.

In fact, the threat of Russia to the economy and security of Europe is direct, and Switzerland is also included in this danger.

Therefore, the sanctions against Iran for sending drones and military weapons must be implemented. The Swiss do not express these goals, and they use the phrase national interests to justify their positions. The reason for making excuses using national interests against human rights violations and massacres is wrong and unacceptable. The arguments of the Swiss government were not and are not sufficient and credible; instead, they were a ridiculous excuse that stained the moral credibility of that country. National interests are not the determinants of any behavior. If national interests are the justifying factor for all actions and positions, there would be no difference between democratic and tyrannical countries or between countries with liberal values and countries with dictatorial values. Any country will make any decision under the pretext of national interests.

The Chinese government also uses the excuse of national interests. It has forced Uighur Muslims in the Xinjiang region into labor camps and violated their freedom of speech and beliefs due to national interests. It has destroyed thousands of Uighur Muslims' places of worship and mosques because Chinese national interests require it. The national security of China is better and more assured by suppressing Uighurs. It signs unclear and unfair agreements with other countries due to national interests, plans heavy loans with high interest rates, and traps weak governments in debt because of the interests of the Chinese. So, they also know the Swiss way, but the Swiss are not even considered to be in the Chinese's shadow using these methods.

The Russian government attacked Ukraine for its own national interests. If the Swiss government were to oppose them and ask: Why did you invade? Why are you destroying civilians and infrastructures in Ukraine? Then, the Russian government can claim its national interests as an excuse. Furthermore, the Swiss government should remain silent because the justification for its silence toward the suppression of Iranian freedom advocates is exactly the same argument that the Chinese and Russian governments use to suppress people and invade countries.

Therefore, the duty is clear and inexcusable for governments that recognize democratic values. On the other hand, there is a front that fundamentally opposes the process of democratic development. They oppose the democratic revolution in Iran, and they also sabotage it. The most prominent examples of them are the governments of China and Russia, both of which support all dictatorships in the world in any possible way to establish authoritarianism.

The amount of support that the Russian government gave to Belarus' dictator Alexander Lukashenko is one example in hundreds of clear cases. After the country's presidential election in 2020, Alexander Lukashenko introduced himself as the president of Belarus for the sixth consecutive time. When the citizens of Belarus protested and expressed their disgust for the management of the country and decades of backwardness on the streets, the security system and suppressive forces began to arrest and attack the people. This attack did not stop, and the commitment and perseverance of the citizens on the streets created intense anxiety in the government – to the point when Lukashenko went to his godfather, Vladimir Putin, and asked for help. The Russian government also openly threatened the people of Belarus, offering the government assistance and dispatch of forces in case of the need for further suppression of the Belarusian citizens.

Russian intelligence and security agencies directly participated in suppressing the democratic movement in Belarus, aiming to prevent Lukashenko from losing power and weakening Russian colonization and its own sphere of influence. Such audacity and interventionist behavior has always been and will continue to be, in countries like these. During the Iranian people's uprising, on 27 October 2022, the Russian government also announced its preparation to cooperate with Iran's anti-terrorism efforts; in other words, the efforts include labeling people on the streets and Iranian protesters as terrorists. The Iranians' threat was interpreted as a fight against terrorism. The Russian government and its security services have experience and expertise in suppressing protesters. Based on this, it attempted to train and assist the military forces of the Islamic government. The military drone regime's gift to kill Ukrainian citizens, and mad men like Vladimir Putin, provide tools and information about complex methods of suppression, serving only the interests of mean dictators.

Other countries oppose the development of democracy in Iran. Oppressive countries in the Middle East, which are considered neighbors of Iran, such as Saudi Arabia, Turkey, Qatar, Pakistan, and others, generally support the establishment of Islamic laws in Iran because the implementation of these laws serves their own desires and goals as well. Qatar has made much effort to establish a Taliban government and strengthened extremists, hasn't it? Is Saudi Arabia seeking to develop democracy by establishing religious schools on a massive scale in Pakistan? They are using the dollars that come from oil and gas sales, along with natural resources, to fund the expansion of Islamism, even at the cost of destroying the hopes and dreams of the citizens.

Although the existence of an Islamic government in Iran would create trouble for neighboring countries, the estimated benefits outweigh the drawbacks. But why? For example, if Iran were to become a democratic and powerful country, Saudi Arabia would no longer be able to control the energy market and the Organization of the Petroleum Exporting Countries (OPEC). Saudi Arabia's totalitarian power as an oil exporter has enabled it to gain extensive influence in global markets and Western countries. The existence of strong competitors would undermine its significant position.

On the other hand, Qatar would not be able to have special privileges and excessive exploitation of the joint gas fields, including the world's largest gas field in the south. With the persistence of the Islamic government in Iran, the development potential of oil and gas fields would be taken from Iran, and major industrial companies would not collaborate to develop the necessary infrastructure for oil and gas extraction. Therefore,

Qatar would continue to benefit from extracting 13 times more oil from the shared fields.

The existence of an Islamic government is also beneficial for Turkey, as it would not have a lucrative tourism industry if there were no Islamic regime in Iran and would have a serious competitor. Such a competitor would limit Turkey's ability to attract investment in the tourism industry. This competitor has both sea and desert, forests, mountains, different ethnic groups and cultures, and countless historical and tourist attractions, so Iran would have the maximum ability to attract tourists, and this would be something of an economic nightmare for Turkey.

With its longing to revive the Ottoman Empire and its uncontrolled military actions in support of Azerbaijan and simultaneous confrontation with Syria, Greece, and Cyprus, Turkey demonstrates a kind of aggressive spirit. Of course, the Turkish government considers a weak Iran more desirable for itself because the existence of powerful and democratic countries goes against its imperialist tendencies. It is easier to reach an agreement between Molla Ali and Erdogan than it is for the true representatives of the Iranian nation and the Islamist Justice and Development Party of Turkey to agree. Dictators usually support each other as they have similar mindsets and common goals.

On the other hand, because of the existence of the Islamic government in Iran, the number of Iranian immigrants is increasing, taking their own expertise and capital with them. Another point is that a democratic revolution in Iran may shake the foundations of its dictatorial regimes, as the courageous and freedom-seeking Iranian people can also spread to other countries.

Countries in the region are familiar with the phenomenon called the Arab Spring, which has engulfed a massive wave of protests and revolutions from North Africa to Oman since 2010. The main slogan was *The people want to overthrow the regime.* Middle Eastern despots have strategically remained silent in the face of the "Woman, Life, Freedom", revolution, as overt support for the massacre and oppression of the Iranian people is not feasible. Moreover, they fear that the Iranian revolution of "Woman, Life, Freedom" may inspire a new vigor and power in the Arab Spring and democratic movements of neighboring countries, especially when considering the inspiring bravery of Iranians. The Arab Spring would be terrifying for Arab sheikhs and backward dictators. The slogans and demands of the Iranians were even more anti-tyrannical than those of the Arab Spring. Kings and government institutions in neighboring countries fear the domino effect of this resistance.

With this description, many countries have not been and are not in favor of the democratic revolution of the Iranian people. In this situation, the people of Iran have utilized their efforts and capabilities to fight against the enemies and forces of the Islamic government by relying on themselves and their own power. The most important aspects of the people's victory over the regime are their self-confidence and relying only on themselves. Of course, this does not mean that the international community has no impact. But, if Iranians persevere and take on the difficulties of the revolution, right when the government changes its decisions in crucial moments, the revolution will not face defeat. If the great Ukrainian people and President Volodymyr Zelensky had surrendered to the invading Russian army on February 24, 2022, or if they were to leave the country, Ukraine would not be able to remain and advance with such strength and bravery. At the same time, the international community was not convinced it should support Ukraine because it argued that a nation that does not defend itself has not left any room for us to defend it.

The Ukrainians remained and showed the world how the concept of a nation takes on concrete form, what the concept of patriotism is, and what the concepts of dignity and bravery are. In these circumstances, the world was convinced that they should defend them in any way possible and began to send them weapons, intelligence assistance, and financial aid.

The difference between the Ukrainians' and Iranians' fights is that Ukraine is fighting against foreign invaders, while the people of Iran are fighting interior invaders. In other words, Iranians are fighting against those who carry out the same terrible behavior as foreign invaders, but the ones they fight are with the guise of being compatriots. Foreign invaders seize the lives, properties, and livelihoods of citizens of a country, while domestic invaders carry out the same behavior under the cover of government and ruling power.

In a classic battle, the enemy is known, and attack and defense have clear meaning, but, in the battle between the Iranian government and the people of Iran, the enemies of the Iranian nation are traitors and anti-human Iranians who have resorted to violence and savagery against the free people of Iran. In this battle between the people and the regime, patriotic Iranians are fighting against traitorous Iranians.

Of course, being Iranian in terms of identity is different from being Iranian in terms of patriotism and nationalism. A person may be born in a country but have behaviors and thoughts that are opposite those of that country, and, at the same time, another person may have lived outside the country for many years, but they have an unbreakable connection to their homeland.

A government composed of people from the same country may be as anti-national as foreign invaders. Because foreign invaders, in the time of takeover, may not want to do the oppression and cruelty more than what they exhibit.

In fact, over the decades of their rule, Mullahs have been able to turn Iran into a burnt forest, worse than foreign invaders, to such a great extent that the amount of damage they have inflicted on the people and the country cannot be measured. Dry lakes and vanished wetlands, a collapsed and crippled economy, along with widespread and debilitating poverty, have been the direct result of their governance. This group is not really Iranian and has taken Iranians hostage for their own interests and empty ideas. Therefore, Iranians are allowed to remove any barriers to their freedom by any means necessary to free themselves from Mullahs. The Iranian people have the right to respond to any threat in proportion to its intensity and level of danger, and they have chosen a controlled form of re-action toward the Islamic government. If people can eliminate the threat of an attacker through dialogue, they will not have the right to use other methods. If there is no need for military weapons to defend the land, then the use of military equipment will not be appropriate. In other words, just as crime and punishment should be proportional, defense and offense should also be proportional. The people of Iran, through no fault of their own, have been placed in an opposing position against the savage Islamic regime.

Such a system is neither democratic nor willing to allow change through peaceful ways. As a result, Iranians are not facing a developed, balanced, or democratic political system. Rather, they face a government that uses violence against even children just minding their own business outside to instill fear and terror and kill its people more easily.

In such conditions, often people see limited options for liberation. They have the right to save themselves from the grip of such a government by using any possible means, like using force or resorting to defense and attacks. The right to resist in such conditions has no negative, unethical, or illegal connotations. Instead, the Iranian people are fully justified in using any possible method to remove the Islamic regime, even if it means the elimination of an enemy front. The lives of the Mullahs and Revolutionary Guards are not an insurmountable obstacle for the Iranian people.

The Mullahs and guards have risked the lives of millions of people and gambled with them, and have willingly become the cause of their own disgrace. If the citizens are seeking to express their objections, opinions, and opposition against that political system, the government has no right – I emphasize it again, *has no right* – to suppress them. People are free and have the right to express their opinions, even if they question the legitimacy and foundation of their government. If the government starts to suppress the people and attempts to use violence with both firearms and cold weapons, the people then have the right to defend themselves. They have the right to stand against oppressive forces and, if necessary, to use proportional violence and defend themselves with all their might in the most effective way possible.

Violence is not inherently negative, just as kindness and civility are not inherently positive. If we have absolute views about these concepts, the problem lies in our perspective because both violence and being pacific can have functional roles. Each of these concepts has consequences for human behavior. The fundamental importance lies in our managing system and appropriately utilizing these two moods and actions in our behavior.

It is not justified to consider human tendencies and acts of violence as inherently discredited as such a perspective undermines the potential for helping the aggressors and dictators, while weakening the potential for the people to lead successful lives. This mindset can even lead to engaging in immorality. In other words, such a position traps ethical individuals in immorality. Expressing opinions regarding the right to use violence should be done with caution and thought. If it was possible to resolve conflicts and solve problems without resorting to violence, then intended paths and non-violent methods should be pursued.

But if people find themselves in a situation where they can't protect themselves without resorting to violence, then using violence is not only justified but necessary. If aggressors attack a country, is reciprocal violence not justified? If someone intends to harm another person and stopping this crime is not possible without violence, is resorting to violence morally wrong? Therefore, individuals who easily perceive violence as contradictory to democracy or ethics do not support the correct position.

A democratic person can use violence as a last resort and tool. However, having the right to use violence does not necessarily guarantee its effectiveness. The effectiveness of violence requires careful consideration of the realities on the ground by decision-makers and strategists of the revolution.

It is advisable to not resort to violence for the betterment of human life. Peaceful and dialogue-based approaches have been designed to reduce suffering and to achieve goals with minimal harm. But this does not mean that if peaceful and dialogue-based approaches are blocked, then humans should become absolute slaves and obedient. The behavior of slavery has no place in the vocabulary of free people. In fact, the inability to express violence does not mean being tolerant. One of the ethical differences among humans is the possession and practice of courage, which shows opposition to oppression and being free. The "Woman, Life, Freedom" revolution is a clear example of such courage. Part of courage also manifests in practical struggle and defense – defense against a government that has blocked all paths of change. Citizens have the right to legitimate defense and can defend themselves against oppressive forces and even attack if necessary. The government appears on the streets with weapons and various military tools, shooting and killing people who raise their voices for their rights and are not accountable to anyone. They are not accountable to the people or even the international community. In such circumstances, the government has waged war against the people, and the people have the right to legitimate defense.

The leader of the Islamic government, amid the "Woman, Life, Freedom" revolution, justifies the suppression of the people with the phrase *hybrid war* (combined war). This blatant admission formalized the war between Iranians and the Mullahs. As the Supreme Commander of the Armed Forces, including the Revolutionary Guards, the army, police, and intelligence agencies, Ali Khamenei openly used the word *war* against the people. This word allows the oppressive forces to consider any kind of violence and brutal behavior permissible against the citizens on the streets. Khamenei, who caused the deaths of thousands of people in the country by banning the entry of the coronavirus vaccine under the pretext of being American and British, has decided to massacre the Iranian people by declaring war against them, using any means and tools available to suppress them.

In the face of terror, defense is not only legal but also necessary. Gentleness and tolerance toward terrorists are as incorrect as resorting to violence against democratic individuals. A government that does not consider a framework for the implementation of people's demands, and suppresses any form of opposition with the most severe and police methods, will not have the right to govern absolutely. People have the right to take appropriate action against such terrorists.

Violence has a harsh and undesirable face, and it will cause harm, but, throughout history, humans have justified the presence of defensive and violent modes. If governments seek order, peace, and public security in society, they must respond to the people's demands and act on their behalf as the owners and rulers of the country. Governments and regimes have no value or weight except through the will and credibility of the people. If the path to the implementation of the people's will is blocked, then the people can overthrow and trash this government by any means necessary.

If governments claim to be advocates of public order and call on citizens to remain silent and obedient under the pretext of public order, it is obviously a deceptive act. If the aim is to establish public order and tranquility, governments should comply with the citizens so that the implementation of affairs does not conflict with order and peace. And if the government does not comply with the citizens, then the people are allowed to use any means to make the government compliant and peaceful. They want to assert their will without resorting to violence. But if changes are not possible without resorting to violence, organized and targeted defense becomes vital. Freedom-loving citizens should organize themselves considering the circumstances and confront the government and its officials without mercy. If they surrender, they should be tried, according to systematic legal rules. This issue is not only related to Iran but rather to people in every society, anywhere in the world; the people should remove hostage-taking governments by any means possible.

Respect, charisma, and the government's grandeur in the face of citizens are the result of outdated thoughts of some people. Presidents and illegitimate ministers have no right to rule, and illegitimate political leaders are the most discredited and criminal individuals and should be eliminated. Xi Jinping, Ali Khamenei, and Vladimir Putin may appear glorious and credible to underdeveloped minds, but they are nothing more than symbols of corruption and cowardice. Grandeur and credibility are reserved for individuals who have the maximum benefit for the citizens of society, show the highest respect and commitment to human rights, and humbly and carefully serve the people of the country. Dictators who seek to suppress people under various pretexts are discredited and deserve no respect. They use everything as an excuse for destroying and eliminating human freedom. They use words like security and order as justification for any kind of action.

The meaning of security and order used by dictators is the safe and uninterrupted exercise of despotism. Their goal and purpose of public order is organizing obedience and public servitude. Dictators' use of words like peace, security, and order means keeping citizens in check and preventing them from disrupting the tranquility and comfort of the ruling class when the time comes for people to disrupt it with their protests.

For dictators, the security of citizens is not important. They make sure they're safe under the guise of public security. Dictators distort the meanings of concepts and replace them with different interpretations. They play with the words' meanings and phrases and use them as a tool to justify their behavior.

For Mullahs, concepts like order, security, peace, friendship, justice, and fairness have a completely different meaning than what ordinary people understand them to mean. They consider killing protesters as justice, and, in reality, the words they use become empty and meaningless, even if the most beautiful vocabulary is employed. They talk about democracy but aim for dictatorship. Whenever they mention homeland, they mean ideological homeland. They use the oppressed word but consider the mobilization forces and thugs as example. They use meaningful words to gain public satisfaction, even though their intended meanings have no connection to the common and conventional meanings of those words.

Therefore, the excuses of dictators using reasonable and widely understood words will not serve as reasons or justifications for their contradictory and heinous behavior.

THE EXCUSE NAMED 'FOREIGN ENEMY'

The perennial excuse that the Islamic regime in Iran uses for controlling and suppressing people, which is always and constantly raised, is the common tool of all tyrants and dictators throughout history, which is foreign intervention and aliens, or just enemies. The purpose of using the word *enemy* with this excuse is to describe the Iranian people, who protest and demand the overthrow of the Mullahs, who are aligned with foreign enemies and enemy countries. Through this, Iranian revolutionaries are portrayed as agents of America and other Western countries. In fact, their goal is to create a basis for strangling and suppressing people so the Mullahs can easily suppress Iranians by labeling them as traitors to their country, of which they are, in fact, true examples.

This method is the most common and oldest excuse of dictators because they introduce themselves as the guarantors of the security and protection of the country and society while also portraying protesting people as subversive and deceived or foreign mercenaries and outsiders.

Joseph Goebbels, who was the minister of public enlightenment and propaganda in Adolf Hitler's government, believed:

"When a government is unable to provide their people with basic needs, such as bread, work, welfare, security, credit, and comfort, in such a situation, the government must divert public opinion toward a secondary but big issue and constantly talk about conspiracy and enemies."

Dictatorial governments that follow the incorrect path do not have the ability or courage to accept responsibility for their actions. For the avoidance of responsibility, they also need excuses and justifications. They don't have a better pretext than creating a fake enemy and exaggerating external threats and foreign interventions. They divert public opinion to an unreal threat and attribute the chaotic situation and deficiencies to the existence of foreign enemies. If the country's economy is on the verge of collapse, or if there is uncontrollable inflation and economic recession, or if the industry and market are stagnant, it's all attributed to the imaginary monster called the *enemy's interference.*

The Mullahs believe that if people in society protest on the streets against the regime, they are considered targets that should be suppressed. Protesters can be eliminated because they are seen as facilitators of enemy plans in the country. They believe that suppressing them is not only necessary but it is also the government's right to protect the country's independence. This kind of deception and the excuses serve the despot's multiple goals simultaneously and can even convince some uninformed parts of society about the political events in the country. Uninformed citizens imagine that, in a situation where enemy, foreign interference, and threats to territorial integrity and national independence are present, the government must impose restrictions and suppress dissenters. They perceive this action as being in the interest of the people's and country's security.

This same form of lies has been one of the main excuses used by the Islamic government to suppress all protests, especially the "Woman, Life, Freedom" revolution. Their entire rhetoric, which revolves around enemy interference, include countries like the United States, Israel, and European nations, rather than China, Russia, and other authoritarian countries. Now, if some people are protesting in the streets, it means nothing to Mullahs except that they think the people are part of the enemy's deception or are agents and mercenaries of Western countries. They interpret the nation's cry for freedom to such an absurd extent. If there is no general and vague concept called the enemy to attribute all the country's problems and deficiencies, then who should be held accountable? They not only have no solutions for problems and backwardness but also lack the courage to accept responsibility for the situation.

One of the main aspects and reasons for highlighting the concept of the enemy is the deep fear that exists within these despots and tyrants. They fear the country's citizens, they fear that their own weaknesses could be exposed, and they fear the consequences that point to the falsehood of their decisions. They do not want to appear weak and always want to strive to appear powerful, flawless, magnificent, and serious. Dictators suppress, torture, humiliate, and violate to prove that they are powerful, when, in reality, the intensity of their fear and terror is unbearable, attacking everything and everyone, to the extent that they even attacked schools and universities during the "Woman, Life, Freedom" revolution. In fact, such madness has multiple reasons, but the dictator's fear of the masses and the decline of his power drive him toward violent actions.

Humans fear losing their possessions. The wealthy fear losing their wealth, the healthy fear losing their health, and the beautiful fear losing their beauty. Such fears can be logically categorized within a framework. However, those who do not have such possessions but steal them from others carry a perpetual fear of losing those possessions or belongings. This kind of fear is different because they do not actually own the capital or property they occupy, and there is always the possibility of losing all their positions at any moment. Therefore, since citizens have the right to reclaim the ruling positions and the properties of the despots whenever they wish, such a situation creates constant fear and terror for dictators.

On the other hand, pessimism, mistrust, and paranoia are among the characteristics of a dictator, to the extent that they feel this way even toward their close friends and associates. One of the factors that led Stalin, the leader of the Soviet Communist Party, to eliminate and expel many of his friends and allies was his extreme pessimism and distrust. With that kind of thinking, he considered everyone and everything to be his enemies, conspirators, and traitors. Any behavior or event is perceived as a plot and conspiracy by such individuals. The Islamic government and regime's leader have been and are trapped in a similar situation. Since the beginning of the Islamic government's establishment, it has eliminated and imprisoned many allies and companions. Anyone who has had the slightest disagreement or different interpretation about the country's management methods has faced ruthless reactions. Such extreme pessimism is clearly evident in the behavior of Ali Khamenei, who imprisoned even his own teachers and professors and eliminated those who played a fundamental role in the formation and strengthening of the Islamic revolution. It is obvious that pessimistic and paranoid dictators will not have a positive relationship with society and the international community. The dictator's pessimism leads to paranoia and a constant sense of conspiracy.

Such a dangerous perspective will pave the way for dark relations with nations, governments, and international organizations, as they categorize all active institutions around the world as enemies and interpret international laws as malicious plots. Therefore, they consider all the plans of such institutions as infiltration that cannot be implemented. For example, the opposition of both the Islamic government and Ali Khamenei to the 2030 Agenda for Sustainable Development Goals, which was an international roadmap for development in the fields of education, human rights, poverty, and gender equality, is a clear example of such an attitude. The reason for the Islamic regime's leaders' opposition was nothing but a sense of enmity and ideological stubbornness.

Ali Khamenei stated the reason for his opposition in a document, *"Here, the basis is Islam, the basis is the Quran. This is not a place where the corrupt and destructive Western lifestyle can influence."*

They imagine everything as planned and designed for infiltration, cutting off from the global community and imprisoning the people of Iran with their false beliefs. They have accepted a book and ideology as the absolute truth and labeled anything contradictory to it as enemy plans and conspiracies. They cannot understand the complexity of the modern world. Their ability to understand the united world and its close communities has diminished. It is not possible to consider everyone as enemies and imprison people in the black hole and underground of the world. Excessive pessimism and the system's hatred toward others will result only in backwardness and seclusion in Marshall McLuhan's global village. Mullahs will consider all dissenters as enemies, including the people and any protesters.

With such a method, propaganda and the repetition of the word enemy and its conceptualization have gradually led government officials to believe that the world is united in enmity and invasion toward Iran and in the attempt to eradicate the personal religion of the people. Rumors and repeated lies have also led them to indoctrinate more to believe in their own falsehoods. The regime has become captive to its own propaganda, as some have become trapped in their own indoctrinations and confirmations, due to excessive repetition, and consider lies as truths.

In a society, where there is no room for dissent and protests, and groups are not allowed to voice their opposition, their own lies become their absolute truth. This propaganda process turns into their genuine belief. On the other hand, as the lifespan of a dictator increases, their mental disorders and mad decisions also increase. The level of a dictator's delusions experienced in the early stages of their rule cannot be compared to how it will be in the later stages of their regime. Throughout their rule, they become so entangled in the whirlwind of lies and one-sided propaganda that they lose the ability to distinguish reality from delusion. Anything they previously believed to be true and certain will be correct, even if the external reality, evidence, and statistics prove otherwise. Their minds cannot accept the tangible outcomes of their decisions.

In the presence of overwhelming evidence, they distort and interpret the matter in a different way to avoid disrupting their previous delusions and fabrications. Their cognitive mistakes become so extensive that they will perceive most obvious issues as harmful, complicated, and twisted. They will consider the most heinous crimes as reasonable and necessary. If they are told that subordinated management institutions are engaging in corruption or crimes systematically based on sufficient and presentable evidence, they will quickly justify it with the exaggeration of a small-scale corruption or denial of corruption altogether, or attribute it to the intervention of foreigners and enemies. Therefore, they block the possibility of dialogue, change, and peaceful solutions, and create the start of social conflict.

TRANSNATIONAL HUMANITARIAN RIGHTS AND INDEPENDENCE OF COUNTRIES

Are international reactions to human rights violations and the suppression of Iranians an example of interference in Iran's internal affairs and a violation of Iranian national independence?

The position of countries regarding government suppressions in countries is justified, and the attention and declaration of positions and proportional reactions by global and governmental organizations against the suppression of Iranian people does not constitute and is not a foreign intervention. That is because the issue of human rights is not a national or territorial matter, but a global and international issue. Before being Iranian, a person is first and foremost a human being. Being a human precedes being Iranian, American, Chinese, or any other nationality. Humans have dignity and validity regardless of nationality. Humans acquire national, social, and familial titles due to the connections they have with their environment. These titles cannot undermine the fundamental rights of humans, as the concept of being human transcends any affiliation or relationship. No institution or government has the right to weaken or attack humans and their rights under any pretext. Therefore, a country's independence does not mean the silence of other countries, regarding genocide, massacres, and human rights violations. Any country that violates the Universal Declaration of Human Rights has already given political and international action permission to other governments and nations. Governments cannot claim that whatever happens in their country is within the realm of national government privacy, so it has no connection to the United Nations, foreign countries, or other nations. They cannot claim that the reactions of other nations and governments constitute interference in their internal affairs. This statement is a baseless and negligent pretext for easier and better implementation of crimes.

Human rights is not an internal or geographical issue, but rather, it is the most fundamental legal document. It is not limited to Iran alone but rather can be valid in any country where human rights violations occur. And, not only can governments and nations show their reactions, but when these proportional reactions are gathered together, they will prevent the occurrence of many crimes. Authoritarian regimes justify the suppression and violation of citizens' rights by utilizing national independence, and they seek to make the international community silent. If other countries have a negative reaction and oppose the atrocities inside another country, it is considered interference in territorial affairs and a violation of national independence.

Dictator political leaders, especially the leaders of the Islamic Republic in Iran, have divided the global sphere into internal and external. They oppress and torture their own people, and if governments or organizations raise objections about Iranian citizens being brutally oppressed, they quickly label that as foreign or enemy interference.

Mullahs and terrorist revolutionary guards introduce war and conflict between the people and the regime as a result of something similar to a family dispute that should be resolved among themselves. This family dispute is used as an excuse or license to silently massacre citizens and demand the silence of other governments and nations. In fact, the relationship between Iranians and the regime is not similar to the connection between a political set and a system. But because of the clash of views between Iranians and the Islamic regime, this resembles the kind of relationship between two enemy fronts.

Members of a political family do not take each other hostage. Instead, they participate and represent in a free and defined relationship, and if the people are dissatisfied, they can be removed from their positions. The conflict in Iran is not a family matter, but rather, it is between the people who are taken hostage and the regime, the hostage taker. The Iranian people fundamentally do not belong to the Islamic government. They do not consider the regime and its leaders as part of their family.

The type of relationship between Iranians and the Islamic government is that of two enemies on a battlefield, each trying to eliminate and weaken the other using any opportunity.

Which family will win the day?

By using deceptive words and portraying them in an unreal space, they attempt to normalize their crimes and fundamental differences for the people to make the Islamic regime and its leaders appear as ordinary matter. Even democratic governments, which are based on the will of the citizens, are obligated to be accountable to the people. What can be said about a government that has taken people hostage and looted their financial and territorial resources by force and with military tools? Mullahs' superficial literature and emotional agitation have no credibility in the political sphere. The people of Iran not only have no tolerance for the Islamic government, but they are also willing to sacrifice their lives for the destruction of it. As seen in the "Woman, Life, Freedom" revolution, the people of the country were killed, tortured, and injured to remove the Islamic government and establish a democratic system. The Iranian nation considers itself to be prisoners in the hands of a psychotic group and must find a way to escape their evil deeds in any form.

Therefore, to relate the unity of behavior and mindset of Iranians with the regime's behavior inside and outside the country is not accurate. If the Islamic regime has an impact on supplying and equipping the Russian army, and if, through these weapons, Russia attacks Ukraine, this is not the viewpoint and demand of the Iranian people. The terrorist behaviors of the regime and Mullahs do not represent the liberal Iranian people's wishes.

The opposition between the people and the government is on a level that even makes many Iranian Muslims resentful of the Islamic government and believe in the removal of the regime, plus the separation of religion and government. The name of the Islamic government should not create false assumptions about the Iranian people. The view that all Iranians are Muslims or all

Iranians are supporters and believers of the religion is neither true nor real. In an isolated system where there is no ability to reflect on intellectual tendencies freely and accurately, determining the exact size and percentage of people's thoughts is impossible. Statistics from impartial institutions that try to recognize tendencies based on scientific methods and approaches and, considering the limitations, will be somewhat expressed. It is not possible to decisively consider even a significant portion of the Iranian people as Muslims, contrary to when some politicians try and present a one-sided image of Iranians by labeling them with abstract titles.

Basically, the existence of religious beliefs being part of Iranian society does not indicate an inclination toward a religious government. A significant portion of religious society in Iran is composed of secular religious people. They are individuals who hold personal and religious beliefs while also believing in the separation of religion and state. From the perspective of the secular Muslims, the Islamic government is illegitimate. Also, many religious people would join the opposition to the Islamic government, including even those who are not secular and believe in theocracy and divine rule. For this reason, in the "Woman, Life, Freedom" revolution, we see a diverse group of protesters, casualties, wounded, and prisoners.

A notable issue is the unity of the people despite their diversity. Different beliefs have not resulted in disruption of collaboration among the Iranian people, and this unity and cohesion has been a nightmare for the Islamic government. Mullahs' threats aim to break and weaken this unity, and they utilize any possibility to disrupt it. People's unity is the main factor for the weakness and defeat of oppressors.

The Islamic regime utilizes techniques like massacre, execution, and spreading rumors to cause division. These ineffective tactics against the people contrast with the unity we saw in the revolution of "Woman, Life, Freedom", which was one of the most unexpected models of national solidarity. For example, Iranians living abroad organized protests that even if they were not unprecedented on a global scale, were really remarkable.

In such a situation, where a nation has risen against tyranny with all its might, global protests by governments and nations are of great importance. Not only must there be protests against oppressive systems, but any government that systematically violates human rights (as it is their usual and perpetual method) must be eliminated by any means necessary, even with appropriate aggression. All rights belong to the people, and illegitimate governments have no rights. Therefore, people, as well as global organizations, should not remain silent in the face of human rights violations and massacres, of any kind, anywhere in the world.

The combination of cries and protests, which aims to protect the value and position of humanity, makes our planet a safer place to live. The voices of others today will be the voice of Iran for others tomorrow. The world's silence in times of suppressing people and violating human rights is the desired behavior of tyrants.

One can watch the actions of Xi Jinping, the illegal president of China, to see his level of fear about the reactions of organizations and other countries and their attention to the systematic flaws of Chinese people's rights. Alternatively, one can observe the fear and apprehension of Vladimir Putin, the illegitimate leader of Russia, to observe his level of aversion to global positions against the massacres in Ukraine or the suppression of the Russian people. Consequently, institutions, organizations, and governments must take a stance against human rights violations, wherever they occur, and act with the circumstances in mind.

Since humanity is beyond nationality and human is beyond the nation, paying attention to fundamental rights is also essential. If a government chooses to be a prison guard instead of being a servant, then it becomes a legitimate target of protest for all other global institutions. In this case, there is no difference between any country or nation. A government without the support of its people has no credibility. Illegitimate governments have no legal authority or validity against or over the people. The dignity and worth of governments depend on their obedience and adherence to their citizens. If governments deviate from this path, then the country's people, along with the global community, have the right to reject them and are entitled to proportionate reactions.

If diplomatic and economic relations between two countries hinder the governments from protesting against human rights violations in another country, then they should be compelled to react for their own people and voters. Nations must be more progressive than governments. There is no rule or principle more important than respecting human rights for all individuals.

Before governments protest against each other's behavior, it is the people and nations of the world who should support and stand with each other. Since governments have always been dangerous and capable of oppression, then throughout history, humans have been under the captivity and control of these governing institutions. Governments need to be compelled to respect, uphold, and be accountable for human rights. Governments have the potential for tyranny and transformation toward dictatorship, so the people of every country should be more progressive than their governments. And, they should be capable of controlling and pushing back political institutions in times of danger and deviation.

Protesting and proportionate reactions against human rights violators are not violations of national sovereignty, and they can restore the independence of countries. Independence of a country in historical definitions is defined as impenetrable, invulnerable, or protection of territorial integrity from another country, or to some extent, self-sufficiency and independence from another country. But independence has a different meaning in today's modern world.

We live in a world that has turned into a small village, where all countries influence, and are influenced by, each other, in an environment where economy, culture, and politics are deeply intertwined. The meaning of independence of a country is defined as its ability to make other countries dependent on itself. When all countries are closely interacting with each other and are dependent on many other countries to meet their needs, the penetration of other countries becomes inevitable. So, a new definition of independence emerges: Any country that creates the highest dependence on other countries to meet various needs and desires will have greater independence.

With such a definition, the Islamic government not only does not have independence, but it has also lost its own independence, according to both the new and old definitions.

Considering the traditional definition of independence, we see that the decisions of China and Russia have a fundamental impact on the policies and decisions of the Islamic government. For example, in the issue of gas extraction, Russia does not allow Iran to extract gas from eight wells because Russia possesses 18.1 % of the world's gas reserves, while Iran has only 17.9 %. If Iran extracts gas from the Caspian Sea, this number would increase to 18.2 % and then surpass Russia. According to agreements between the Islamic government and Russia, Russia must still be at the forefront of gas extractors. As a result, Iran does not have permission to extract its own natural resources due to pressure from Russia. Such an event can be described only as the lack of independence of a country.

With the new definition of independence, the Islamic regime has nothing to offer but to bind other countries to itself, except oil and gas, which are among the free natural resources and are not the result of the efforts, planning, and diligence of the Islamic government. However, due to destructive policies and efforts to build nuclear bombs, Western sanctions have prevented Iran from exporting its resources out of the country. As a result, the global market has managed the shortage of Iran's oil and gas exports. Other countries, such as Saudi Arabia and Qatar, took on the responsibility of providing the required fossil fuels. Iran's share in the global economy and market has diminished. Therefore, due to the oppressive governing of extremist Mullahs, independence is negated in the new sense of the word.

Having independence does not mean turning a country into a prison and killing its prisoners silently while the global community is silent. If parents subject their child to beating, individuals close to the incident must intervene and prevent it. This reaction does not mean unwarranted interference in the parent's relationship with their children. It is simply that parents, despite their closeness and kinship with their children, do not have the right to engage in violence against their children or behave in such a way that violates children's rights.

If they commit such an act, others not only have the right to intervene and react but are also obligated to do so. In this case, parents cannot say: *"Why are you interfering? It's our own child, and we can behave however we want."* Such talk is not justified or acceptable, by any means, especially when it comes to children and their parents, who have the closest kinship relationship. The situation is much more complex when it comes to governments because governments have no right to exercise any form of power unless it is according to the will of the citizens. If they suppress the people of the country, then proportional interventions by other countries and international institutions are justified and do not violate the country's independence.

COUNTRY'S LAWS AND RULE-BREAKER REVOLUTION

In most countries around the world, there are constitutional laws, which serve as the highest legal articles. These laws are designed to maintain public order, uphold individuals' rights, and organize the affairs of the country. The main goal of the legislation is to provide comprehensive and consistent service to the citizens of a society. It is necessary to have individuals who consider the needs and rights of the people in various aspects and strive to fulfill them and solve problems through expertise, commitment, and the use of legal tools. Therefore, the following two main topics are very important:

1. law, and
2. legislators

Validating factors and legitimizing characteristics are important because any group or laws that have not gained the necessary credibility from the people lack authority in the legislative domain. Legislators should be chosen freely by the people under democratic conditions to represent the people. If such a process does not happen, legislators will have no legitimacy for legislation. Their behaviors and official statements will not completely reflect the views of the community.

Furthermore, laws should not contradict the Universal Declaration of Human Rights and should not undermine the interests and rights of the people. However, if they do, the law will be invalid and can't impose any obligations for people to comply with it.

Being legitimated needs various but connected factors and reasons. It is not a function of separated elements. The law does not take shape in a vacuum or abstract space. Rather, it must be approved based on public benefit and within specific and systematic frameworks. For example, if a government officially approves racist laws and designates them as legally binding citizens' duty, it is not obligatory to follow such a law, and fighting against it becomes an important ethical and civic duty.

If the enacted laws cause the suppression of a portion of the people and violate citizen's rights, then ignoring and violating such laws becomes the citizens' most important political behavior. Essentially, laws are mechanisms that guarantee the rights of individuals within the framework of a nation-state. If fighting against incorrect and unjust laws was not legitimate, all the anti-human laws of the past would have remained, and no positive change would have occurred in human life.

If there had been no opposition to the discriminatory laws in America by such pioneers as Rosa Parks, Martin Luther King Jr., and their like-minded people, those unjust and wrong laws would have remained in place or become worse. However, the main point is that there are established mechanisms for changing bad laws, and the political system anticipates the possibility of transforming and altering wrong laws. In such circumstances, the incorrect law should be swiftly repealed using the designated paths. And if such paths are not specified and the possibility of removing the wrong law is eliminated, then comprehensive opposition by citizens remains the only correct way of action.

The rule of law is an important principle in governing a country. For a law to have legitimacy, it must arise from a popular and democratic parliament. If the use of law becomes a justification for officials to impose their personal opinions under flimsy pretexts, then the rule of law is violated, and the enforcement of the law in such a case becomes a manifestation of social bondage and slavery. Breaking such laws is the most justified and desirable behavior.

Dictators claim that a country needs order and that order is based on law, so the laws we declare are mandatory and inviolable. This justification is fundamentally incorrect because not every form of order is desirable, and not every law is correct. If order is based on law, then what must be clarified is which model of order is based on which type of law.

The desired order of dictators is a form of obedience of enslaved citizens to oppressive structures. Correct order should aim to secure the interests of the people with the least restrictions. An order that strengthens and fulfills the rights and interests of the people becomes the desirable order. Therefore, not every model of order and not every law should be the criterion for people's obedience.

Iranians have also witnessed the suppression of their protests under the pretext of law. All the unjust laws that existed in the country, have been justified by the use of law. Any individual who opposes the enforcement of such laws is labeled as a rule-breaker and lawbreaker citizen. In reality, one must either submit to the Mullahs' brutal laws or engage in law- and structure-breaking resistance.

During a revolutionary movement against a corrupt structure, both civil disobedience and defensive or offensive actions may appear harsh. Breaking the law becomes an inevitable occurrence in both forms of struggle. And a law's illegitimacy will be unfolded by the citizens. Essentially, the revolution means breaking the structure. People who seek to overthrow a political regime have risen against its integrity. Is it possible for an oppressive political structure to collapse without breaking the law?

If the wrong law and wrong structure are eradicated through political and civil activities, then, of course, the citizens will violate fewer laws. Otherwise, an oppressive regime can be removed through maximum law-breaking actions. In democratic countries, individuals who do not believe in democracy may come to power, such as former U.S. President Donald Trump and former president of Brazil Jair Bolsonaro; they cannot change all the laws and are ultimately sidelined by the people through the next elections by peaceful means. This process would be less costly and better. But many systems and dictators can't be removed in such a way because they exert control over the people through direct repression and intimidation. In this situation, breaking the laws and regulations to the maximum extent and engaging in a revolutionary act of breaking the structure will be the most ethical and justifiable action.

If the laws are discriminatory and wrong, they should not be enforced by the citizens of the society as much as possible. For example, if the laws of the Islamic regime introduce half of a man's share of inheritance compared to a woman's, men should not adhere to this law; they consciously and willingly share an equal portion with women. Lack of commitment and disobedience to the wrong law is one of the effective methods of civil disobedience.

In the process of the "Woman, Life, Freedom" revolution, the people of Iran are allowed to break the law because the regime's wrong and discriminatory laws have no legitimacy. Laws that deprive citizens of their rights have no validity. For a hostage, hostage-taker's laws have no credibility. The Mullahs' oppressive political system has no capacity for change unless through law-breaker actions. A comprehensive attack on all parts of such government is justified, legitimate, and authorized. Restrictive laws of this regime are discredited and should be dealt with as aggressors.

Neither Thomas Hobbes's perspective nor Immanuel Kant's approach in his book, *The Metaphysics of Morals*, and both are in favor of government, with analytical differences, is correct in this situation.

But the correct view belongs to John Locke, who considers the overthrow of a government as an inalienable right of the people. He believes that the essence of government is created from a contract between the people and should guarantee the natural rights of citizens. Therefore, whenever a government, regardless of its structure and origin, violates the natural rights of citizens, it is essentially declaring war against its own people, and its legitimacy is then void. In such circumstances, Locke believes that overthrowing the government is an inherent right of the people.

This theory is clearly reflected in the Declaration of Independence of the United States, which says: *"Life, liberty, and the pursuit of happiness are the undeniable rights of the people, and whenever any form of government becomes destructive of these rights, it is the right of the people to alter or abolish it and to institute a new government that will secure their rights."*

With this description, if a country is under attack, its people can defend their land by any means necessary and will not allow the enemy to invade and dominate. The goal of foreign enemies is plunder and invasion, the exploitation of the country, and the looting of its resources and capital, which is exactly what the Islamic regime is doing.

The title of internal or foreign aggressors does not have any impact on the comprehensive fight against invaders and occupiers. If the invaders and oppressors of the nation were among the people of the country, they would be treated the same way as foreign invaders. There is no difference between Saddam and Khamenei. The Iranian people have the right to remove the Islamic fascist regime from power in any way possible, just as they stood against Saddam and his invasion and defended their homeland and lives.

Breaking the chains of the Islamic regime's laws will be necessary in this path.

If these excuses are used: *"The law does not permit"*, *"The law prohibits it"*, or *"What is the authority of the law?"*

Then, the answer must be: *"It is obvious that the law prohibits it but the prohibition of the laws, which derived from the Mullahs' parliament, is invalid, and the occupier lawmaker must be fairly tried."*

The success of the revolution against the Islamic regime in Iran will undoubtedly come from breaking these laws because none of the Islamic government's laws allow freedom and democracy for the people. Even the smallest attempt to bring about change has been declared illegal. Therefore, passing through the Islamic government without breaking the laws that are designed to control the people would be a fantasy. The people, regardless of the brutal laws of the Islamic Consultative Assembly (its representatives officially announced that *they demand the execution* of Iranian protesters), can break the laws of the Islamic government and move toward establishing an alternative order and achieving progress with all their might.

A law that was created to weaken and humiliate the people is a law of prison. Breaking such a law is both right and necessary. In the past, slavery was legal, and human trafficking and buying and selling children were also legal. People were enslaved and exploited under these laws. The enslaved had no right to oppose. It was obvious that, if the slaves resisted, then that action went against the prevailing tradition and exploitative law and would undoubtedly upset the slave owner. Those who benefited from profit were clear in their intention to continue slavery under the pretext of the law. But such laws did not prevent them from breaking the structure of slavery and, later, the liberation of human beings from bondage. Also, the opposition of Iranians and all the requirements of their revolution are legitimate, lawful, and ethical. With the commitment to the principles of human rights, there are no limitations on breaking the oppressive laws of the Islamic regime.

ETHICAL LIFE AND BEING A REVOLUTIONIST

The process of revolution against totalitarian regimes will involve a specific and distinct approach compared to other political systems. Of course, it is not possible to envision a singular path or method for all societies and political conditions but instead, the approach will be justified and effective, or unjustified and ineffective, depending on the type of governments, political conditions, and popular potential.

If a political regime does not provide an alternative for change other than a comprehensive revolution, then such a process will inevitably contain violent and distressing scenes. Amid such a defensive and offensive scene, it is normal for repressive forces to engage in attacks and defense against citizens. They will attempt to control the people through various crimes, and numerous unpleasant incidents will occur. In response, the people will defend themselves. This cycle of repression and defense, which is erosive and reciprocal, will be violent, and it is different from the usual frameworks of peaceful and dialogue-oriented approaches.

Regardless of whether people unquestionably have the right to defend or attack an illegitimate government, because they have this right for sure, and regardless of the separate or simultaneous legal and ethical aspects, can revolutionary violent behaviors that result in killing or injury of government forces or repressive powers be considered a subset of unethical actions?

I answer this question with a reference to Germany's national hero, Johann Georg Elser. He was a German carpenter, who attempted to assassinate Hitler and other Nazi leaders. He knew that the Nazi leaders gathered together every year for a memorial celebration at The Bürgerbräukeller hall, in the city of Munich. He had made a time bomb to assassinate Hitler and hid at the location for several days to reach his target. On November 8, 1939, due to a change in the schedule caused by bad weather, Hitler's speech started half an hour earlier, and he left the session earlier than expected. The bomb exploded 13 minutes later. Out of the 200 people present, eight were killed, and 63 were injured. Elser was arrested while illegally crossing the Swiss border and was imprisoned for five years without trial. Eventually, in April 1945, he was executed at the Dachau concentration camp.

President of Germany Frank-Walter Steinmeier expressed appreciation for those who resisted against the Nazi regime on the 75th anniversary of the unsuccessful attempt on Hitler's life on 8 November 1939. The president of one the most democratic countries in the world said the following about Johann Georg Elser's attempt on Hitler's life:

"We all know that there was not much resistance, but there were brave individuals who did not turn a blind eye to what was happening and preserved their humanity. They supported those under persecution and opposed the crimes of the Nazis. The final efforts of those who resisted and sought to end the ruthless war and the rule of the Nazi regime came at the cost of their lives and the lives of their supporters. The respect that should have been given to these courageous individuals has been neglected for a long time, despite the fact that they are an important part of the history of German liberation. Their courage is unforgettable to us."

The direct and explicit answer is that I believe that violent behavior, even in the form of aggression rather than defense, is completely moral and good if the circumstances make it necessary. In fact, it will be among the most justifiable and ethical manifestations of human action.

The point is that the appearance and face of behaviors do not determine their positive or negative morality charge. Just as laughing and being happy or crying and mourning are not considered appropriate in all situations; their desirability is determined by their suitability to the conditions and circumstances. The same rule applies to human behavior. Absolutism in morality is not the solution because, just as unreasonable violence is negative, senseless kindness is wrong too. In other words, ethics is about fitting human behavior to existing conditions to increase well-being and reduce pain and suffering.

If we talk about kindness or violence, it can't be said that kindness is always preferable everywhere because it seems milder and more pleasant. While violence is always extreme and wrong because it has an aggressive and unpleasant appearance. If violence is used correctly and in the right situation, it can be considered good. The presence of anger and the use of violence in certain situations may be the most necessary action possible. One of the important tools for the survival and well-being of intelligent humans is the use of psychological and behavioral states of anger and violence to respond appropriately to environmental threats.

The methods of threats change over time with the evolution of humans and the complexity of societies. If something was perceived as a threat 5,000 years ago, it may not be considered a danger in the present era, and vice versa. Something that we perceive as a threat in the 21st century may not have been a concept or reality in the past, and it may remain the same in the future. For example, global warming, climate change, and greenhouse gas emissions lead to warmer temperatures, droughts, wildfires, heavy rainfall, and rising sea levels, which pose a serious threat to humanity. However, in the past, the concept of global warming did not even exist. In the past, humans would lose their lives to the weakest viruses and diseases, but in the present era, such diseases have become unimportant and eradicated.

Therefore, the form and basis of threats will be different, and human responses will be proportional to the type of threat.

One of the serious threats against humans is governments and states. In past societies that had a local, ethnic, and tribal structure, the model of social management was simpler. Over time, as societies became more complex, control and management systems also became more complicated. Particularly, governments emerged equipped with deadly weapons, technological tools, surveillance, tracking, and control, which increased the level of infiltration, violence, and control.

In the face of complex political regimes, there is no path except comprehensive and intelligent confrontation with them. Although utilizing these methods seems unpleasant, they will not have any moral prohibition. Proper violence in the field of combat with dictators is not equivalent to being emotional or irrational. Just as the concepts of reason and anger can be incompatible, they can also have the potential to be compatible. Therefore, acting timely and with proportional anger is both ethical and logical.

Timely and proportional anger, which, when planned against totalitarian governments, are the most necessary and effective political behaviors because a regime, like the Islamic government, interprets pacifism as passivity and civility as consent from the government. In a period when people engage in civil activities, security forces and regime mercenaries are busy identifying and planning to eliminate active and influential individuals. Civil activities, despite their positive impact, are ineffective in overthrowing the Islamic regime. Without a doubt, proportional violence against the beasts of the Islamic regime will result in the killing, injuring, imprisoning, and torturing of some fighters and people.

People who are aware of the dangers ahead along the path of freedom will sacrifice themselves, risking their lives for the sake of attaining freedom and justice, demonstrating the purest form of humanity and ethics. In fact, fighting in any form against oppressive regimes is the most ethical behavior possible. An individual who confronts the Islamic government and knowingly sacrifices his or her life for the attainment of freedom and the rights of the nation is a symbol of courage and freedom.

Reaching the peaks of welfare and happiness for all nations has been difficult. Such a path is not a direct and smooth road; it's a rough road, full of ups and downs. At every stage of this process, one must behave according to the situation. The person, who writes and speaks in the heart of the democracies to advocate for freedom, and the revolutionary citizen, who fight in the town squares and streets to break the structure of tyranny, are acting ethically. However, an individual who will pay a higher price displays a more valuable ethical behavior. They are simultaneously aware of the price they pay, and at this point, many retreat because living and survival are important and valuable to humans. Individuals who put their lives and existence on the battlefield against the evil of governing power and fights for freedom and human rights have sacrificed themselves and their existence for their ideals. These can't be compared to any other ethical behavior. Devotion and sacrifice for a noble goal will not happen except by a dignified human being. They are noble, and honor gains its meaning from them.

If someone provides financial assistance to others, even a little, this behavior is judged more easily and quickly. They say, *"Such an act is considered a good and ethical behavior."* However, if an Iranian uses violence against the oppressive forces of the Islamic regime to achieve freedom and liberation, some people hesitate to call it correct and ethical behavior.

But for individuals who are engaged in the fight against the regime and sacrifice their lives in the face of terrorists, their behavior will be much more noble and ethical than providing financial assistance to others. The cost of these two actions can't be compared in any way. However, since the appearance and form of one behavior are sympathetic and the other is harsh, it creates reasons for doubt and hesitation in some people.

If the people's revolution can be successful by eliminating the corruption factor, any proportional action that is in line with this goal is ethical and good. But the goal is not absolute and boundless violence. For this reason, the word proportional is always mentioned as a condition. It is obvious that blind violence is wrong, but proportional violence aimed at removing the Islamic government needs to be reasonable and rational.

If, without resorting to violence, the regime is overthrown, for instance, with the extensive presence of millions of people, there would be no need for violence. The important issue is a comprehensive and coordinated fight, considering the circumstances and the legitimacy of any form of necessary battle, against the Islamic regime. Any revolutionary behavior, whether through writing, speech, or field battle, is necessary and ethical. However, determining which action is in line with the revolution or which behavior constitutes extremism is another subject that depends on various factors.

In the process of revolution, excesses or deficiencies will occur, and there is no escape from them. Naturally, some inappropriate behavior and unforeseen incidents will happen, but such occurrences should not have any impact on advancing the course of the revolution. Instead, all efforts and focus should be on reducing uncontrolled events while simultaneously launching a comprehensive and powerful rebellion against the oppressive Islamic government.

The possibility that defensive action on the battlefield may include violent forms is an inevitable result of the political battle with the beasts of the Islamic regime. In normal circumstances, democratic citizens have no means other than law and dialogue.

The fact that such freedom-loving individuals have been forced to resort to unconventional methods is the compulsory result of the struggle against the Mullahs' regime and its filthiness. This is just like when Ukrainian students and professors, who were studying and teaching in Ukrainian cities, were forced to use weapons and ammunition on the battlefields when Russia invaded Ukraine.

They turned theory into action and aligned the world within their minds with the reality of the country. They preferred sitting in trenches over the comfort and luxury of chairs.

Revolutionary Iranians and individuals, who have begun the fight against the historical tyranny of the Mullahs, have followed such a path. Their behavior reflects ethical truths. They are the reason for pride and the spread of truth-seeking in the world. Iranians are the display of courage and a longing for freedom. They have shown sacrifice and devotion with all they possess in the face of beasts whose cruelty was unimaginable even for governments and nations, so much so that well-known politicians expressed their astonishment, from official government tribunes about the behavior of the Islamic regime and its direct massacre of the people.

In essence, revolutionary ethics entail standing against evil and wrongdoing. In a moment when a person turns a blind eye to his or her possessions, sacrifice gains meaning.

For this reason, individuals who sacrifice their lives defending people and their country are always considered the most eternal and respected members of society. People witness their devotion and sacrifice. They have taken actions that not everyone is capable of. This incapability is understood by the people in the society.

Many people are not willing to give up any of their possessions. They are not eager to help and support others. They seek all benefits and individuals for themselves and to serve their own interests, even if they do adhere to ethical behavior in some cases, it is for their immediate personal gain. For this reason, everyone admires the astonishing sacrifice of the revolutionary man or woman on the path of freedom, democracy, human rights, and defense of the people. Sometimes, an act in the revolution may be seen as extreme violence by some and perceived as reasonable violence by others.

The issue is that having differing opinions on what behavior constitutes extreme violence does not harm the essence of the revolutionary movement. The path and goal of the revolution of democratic Iranians is rational and precise, and even if excesses were to occur, it should not destabilize the foundation of the revolutionary movement. Determining what actions are extreme violence is clear in some cases. But in many situations, it requires accurate and comprehensive information about the circumstances and understanding of the battle structures of both sides of the conflict. Without such information, labeling an act as extremist will be equally unethical and inappropriate.

The level of required violence is determined by the strategists of the revolution and the fighters in the streets based on the current conditions. Maybe someone, who is sitting in the comfort of their home and beside a fireplace, believes that violence is necessary to advance the revolution to a certain extent, but military leaders and combatants against oppressive forces may set different boundaries.

In the operation to retake the occupied cities in Ukraine, such as Kherson, Ukrainian forces knew that civilians could be killed or injured. But does the mere occurrence of such incidents and possibilities mean that the country should be used to invading Russians?

The answer to that is *no* because, in war, there will be mistakes and casualties. Civilians and children will be threatened, but the situation in occupied territories is not normal or conventional. Some places, similar to Kherson, did not have the security and normalcy of other cities in the world. The security in somewhere like Paris or Tokyo did not exist in Kherson. Therefore, the behavior of citizens in these two different worlds will not be the same. The law-abiding and non-violent behavior of a French citizen in Paris will not be the determining model for the behavior of a Ukrainian in a war situation facing Russian invaders in Kherson. Failing to differentiate between those two environments is a big mistake.

The utmost effort in revolutionary and wartime situations is to minimize damage to revolutionaries and the people while inflicting maximum harm on the enemy. Implementing such a strategy is a crucial responsibility.

The humanistic laws and principles that the democratic revolutionaries believe in should not prevent them from engaging in effective combat against oppressors. They must fight the murderers of the nation mercilessly while respecting the framework of human rights. Compassion in the fight against oppressive governments means defeat, and defeat means asking for mercy. Just as after victory, trial and adherence to the law are among the most important behavioral principles of democracy advocates; serious and comprehensive fight should be the rule and method during the battle. If such a serious and courageous battle, which may appear violent, is the only remaining option against the beasts of the Islamic government, then people have the right to act according to their judgment and ability. The path to less pain and suffering in human life is through pain and suffering, but without enduring that pain and bearing suffering, one will neither succeed nor reach the desired goal.

WOMAN, LIFE, FREEDOM

The slogan and profile of the Iranian revolution are both so deep and magnificent that facing it alone is sufficient for approval. Even the officials of the Islamic regime were unable to oppose it. They approved the slogan while adding an Islamic interpretation to it, emptying the words of their meanings and appropriating them according to their usual method. The chosen words in this slogan are so precise and full of meaning that, in the initial stage, they seem insignificant, but then, you'll be amazed and enjoy such a selection and arrangement. It is a short but meaningful slogan. I had not seen a more meaningful and beautiful slogan than "Woman, Life, Freedom". And it is an honor to be associated with such a valuable and progressive movement. In fact, it quickly became global because of the depth and truth hidden within it. The minds and souls of people accept the evident truth. Most people are not opposed to the truth but sometimes get trapped in environmental influences or the dust of their own concepts.

In fact, the "Woman, Life, Freedom" slogan represents points and topics that are meaningful to Iranians, plus it also has a significant connection to people in different countries. Therefore, many societies have embraced this slogan, feeling a sense of belonging and connection to such ideals. The issues of women, quality of life, and the principle of freedom, which is the vital element, are the most fundamental needs of human beings for behavior and making decisions. People in various countries found themselves identifying with the concepts of the Iranian revolution because they were aware of the value and importance of the three concepts in their own lives and felt the significance of being connected to a human revolution.

If a nation rises up for human rights, other individuals will also feel a sense of connection and belonging due to the same values inherent in these rights. All humans, as individuals, demand the realization of their rights, and the absence and deprivation of these values undoubtedly signal the destruction of life.

Humans have an understanding of their own needs and suppression is distressing. If people around the world were to witness individuals who are under oppression, striving to reclaim their rights while demonstrating sacrifices and dedication, it would be natural for them to feel a sense of connection to the fighters on the path of freedom and to evaluate their revolution in terms of human dignity and human rights. We would also feel a sense of belonging to the people who strive and sacrifice for human values and their own rights.

Many people in the world have tasted the suffering and pain of living in societies that are not free. Women in various countries have experienced, and *continue* to experience, too much gender discrimination. In the collective memory of most individuals, people who are existing, not living, with everyday struggles and exhausting endurance lack the flow of a great life, through no fault of their own.

An individual who has experienced the pain and suffering of living in difficult conditions will have a better understanding of the very distressing circumstances of others. That is why people around the world felt a sense of connection to the powerful and meaningful slogan of "Woman, Life, Freedom" as they have experienced the exhausting challenges of rights violations and the absence of freedom in various proportions.

Since "Woman, Life, Freedom" refers to a global issue, it has become a global slogan. However, the attention of citizens will vary on a broad scale because everyone's level of concern is not the same, in terms of human values and their own rights.

One of the influential factors in the perspective of individuals toward events and occurrences is the extent of their positive and negative experiences throughout life. The level of identification with and understanding of the deprivations of the disadvantaged class is not feasible for those in privileged positions, and if so, their understanding of those issues would be quite minimal.

Understanding and comprehending the difficulties is almost impossible without lived experience. For this reason, among all the individuals around the world who hear "Woman, Life, Freedom", none of them would have the same imagination and understanding of it. It is impossible for a woman born in Norway or Finland to truly grasp the suffering of oppressed women in the Middle East; she can only imagine and have a general perception. She thinks about how it would feel if she couldn't choose her own attire, but she will still have a superficial understanding of the issues. In other words, those who have tasted the bitterness of discrimination in their daily lives and endured constant oppression will have a deeper and more genuine understanding of the cry for "Woman, Life, Freedom". In any case, whether it is superficial imagination or genuine understanding, it has always been a tool for feeling a sense of belonging to a humanistic uprising.

This slogan and the concepts contained within it were an inspiring expression of the truth-seeking of the Iranian people. Simply put, the demands of people in other countries were also being voiced through the mouths of Iranians. They felt that what the Iranians were saying they wanted was what those in other countries also wanted.

How is it possible that Iranians can stand up courageously and bravely against bullets and torture? How are the people able to rise up against a government that has engulfed the Middle East in its atrocities, yet they do not retreat from their ideals and goals? What is hidden in the content of this demand and this path that an Iranian would die for, but *not* step back, in the pursuit of such an ideal? They also desire freedom, a better life, and equal rights for women. If such an event were to take place in Europe or the United States, it would be considered a pioneering movement, but the "Woman, Life, Freedom" revolution emerged right from the heart of Iran, indicating the level of avant-garde thinking among Iranians.

The slogan is a showcase and reflection of consciousness. People who center their slogan around women and women's rights, people who declare freedom and liberation from restrictions as the basis of their demands, and citizens who seek a humane and desirable life have shown their understanding and perception of their desired kind of world through the slogan.

Some may revolt, but they may pursue backwardness and misguided ideals as their goal of struggle, as has been experienced by many, and many others have paid high prices in the many protests and revolutions throughout history. Many individuals were killed in the pursuit of realizing Communist governments, but their efforts (not necessarily heartfelt intentions) have been toward the contrary goal of well-being and prosperity of society. Essentially, they fought for years to try and change oppressive governments, but due to the lack of correct content or the fanciful nature of the idea they were pursuing, they not only failed but also gambled human lives with their ineffective ideologies.

Revolution and fundamental transformations require not only a fight against the political regime but also the need for alternative content and meaning. The dismantled system must be replaced with a different structured order. The alternative system, in addition to its form and shape, requires correct content and ideals. The principles and goals of the revolution are the most vital part of the process. Setting and formulating such a goal requires great precision and a deep understanding of the living conditions of humans in the ideal society. It is necessary for the principles and goals of the revolution, while being feasible, to be based on human rights. A subject can be correct, but not feasible, just as a subject can be feasible, but not correct. Attention to all dimensions of cases and possibilities is essential.

The main slogan in revolutions and protests refers to a meaning that reflects the fundamental problem of society. If, in a democratic country, the slogan is against inflation and disproportionate price increases, it is an economic issue and a reflection of the people's declining purchasing power. But in a country where people are fighting against an oppressive, illegitimate regime, the essence of their outcry is different and completely distinct.

They are not demanding partial or structural reforms. Rather, they do not want the foundation of such political systems and are searching for an entirely alternative model in the absence of the established regime.

The slogan "Woman, Life, Freedom" is a structure-breaker cry against the Islamic regime. It is a rebellion to reclaim all lost rights and a reflection of the discrimination and deficiencies that have affected all members of society. The issue declares a suffocating and disheartening life that has broken the spirits of Iranians. In fact, in a society without freedom, nothing exists. Freedom is central to human life. An individual who cannot pursue his or her desires is empty of enthusiasm and meaning, spending their days in a monotonous and futile manner, all because they are denied the fundamental basis of social life – freedom.

Of course, for the slaves and people who are not committed to any principle or value, it certainly doesn't matter if there is no freedom or how they continue their empty lives. They are born to inhale oxygen and exhale carbon dioxide for some time, constantly taking a position on the side of falsehood and wrong front, ensnaring others with their irresponsibility. They do not realize the impact of their behavior on social life and their own future and society. But in front of them, some individuals do not want to accept that kind of life, saturated with a sense of captivity. They understand life, freedom, and human rights, and that prevents them from wanting a life living in imposed captivity. They demand tyranny to end and they want the experience of liberation and want to breathe in freedom any way they can. They seek to break the restrictive frameworks that have turned the country's citizens' lives into a playground for empty political or ideological illusions. They cannot see themselves as extraneous forces of the delusions and wicked plans of a few. Their conscientiousness and dignity prevent them from surrendering and subjugation.

Even if advertisements, media, and the Mullahs' education system had surrounded the people who want better lives, these methods haven't been able to change their thoughts and desires. Despots imprison people's bodies and take lives, but they don't have absolute control or access to their thoughts. By presenting one-sided advertisements, the regime creates a basis for enslaving the people, but the rulers of human existence are still themselves. Iranians have shattered all the infrastructures and imposed ideas of the Islamic regime. Their external and secular revolution was the result of an inner revolution. Since thought is the basis of action and thought precedes behavior, the revolutionary behavior of the Iranian people is undoubtedly the result of a revolutionary thought that has already occurred. The shout for freedom and the grandeur witnessed in the streets were the result of the progressive thoughts of Iranians. Breaking incorrect traditions, the courage to liberate from imposed governmental ideologies, and embracing modernity were prerequisites for the realization of the revolution of "Woman, Life, Freedom", which had already taken place.

The people of Iran are strongly crying out that they do not want the Islamic government, and they have shown this unwillingness in various ways.

For example, the confession of Pouyan Hoseinpour, the deputy of the Seraj Sepah Organization, on October 31, 2022, is evidence of the level of people's disgust with the Islamic regime:

"This generation is not afraid of being beaten; it resists. Yesterday, we were engaged in clashes on the streets for an hour. Formerly, when we attacked, they would retreat, but this time, they stand. When we enter certain alleys, every 30 buildings [they] throw stones at us or throw flowerpots and irons at us."

The heightened level of people's disgust against the Islamic regime is undeniable, and the people's hatred toward the regime signifies a revolution, not a demand or protest. If individuals claim that the revolutionary uprising of the people is for reformation, then, in fact, they are taking a position against the people because this is clearly different. It is evident in the recognition of the Iranian people's revolution by the President of france Emmanuel Macron and the betrayal of the spokesperson of the U.S. State Department, Ned Price, who referred to the people of Iran at the same time as they are seeking reforms! The people of Iran are certainly not waiting for confirmation or denial from others, but betrayal is always a painful scene.

If some were to sacrifice their lives for freedom while others are concerned only with securing economic interests and hiding or distorting the prevailing truth before the eyes of the world, that would be unforgivable.

When Iranians cry out for *women*, they want to show a normalized crime against half of the citizens of society, to recount the madness of the government that has restricted them from their basic rights, from women's clothing to their political activities, which are limited. The gender apartheid system has not neglected any restrictive laws against women. The Islamic regime has deprived half of the people of society of their most natural and fundamental rights under the sole pretext of gender. The meaning of the "Woman, Life, Freedom" slogan in the Iranian revolution is different from the concept understood in many other countries. The fight against gender discrimination in Iran, similar to what is happening in some democratic countries, is not just about demanding more rights but about the lack of basic rights and equality for women and girls to begin with.

From childhood, women are controlled in the most restrictive form by using traditions and religious teachings. They invade the minds of girls and create gender stereotypes in their unconscious and conscious. They make female children believe that they are different from men, and because of their differences, they need limitations, and that being social and competitive is not suitable for them. With flimsy excuses, they oblige women to adhere to a particular type of clothing and behavior. They determine fixed social roles for them that are unchangeable. Since the day they are born, women grow up within the boundaries of a concept called *guardianship* for women, which, before marriage, deals with her father and paternal grandfather, and after marriage, it then pertains to her husband. In practice, women do not experience any individual independence in their lives. The Islamic regime has regulated all laws in such a way that women remain trapped in the prison of its antiquated customs and laws.

To make the impact of the guardianship mentality of Mullahs clearer, I will provide an example. In the current legal system in Iran, a woman cannot independently apply for a passport without her husband's permission. But why does such a law exist? In the religious beliefs of the Mullahs, independence for women is not considered.

When it is said that fathers and husbands have guardianship over women, it means that women are prohibited from making any decisions independently! The husband's consent form, which is required for obtaining a passport, is due to the same guardianship derived from religious ideologies. Within the concept of guardianship, the mother has no place because she is a woman and can't have that place. In the discriminatory meaning of guardianship, there is also a hidden discrimination. Therefore, fathers and husbands have the right to control women. They can issue many permits for many matters related to women or reject them as they wish. With this simplicity, the lives of millions of people are played with and somehow justified by the laws of a few who consider themselves representatives of an abstract concept called God. Some are deprived for flimsy reasons, while others are privileged.

For years, they have believed in everything in an absolute and extreme way. As a result, they cannot think differently or accept the concepts of the modern world. They see men and women as having completely different rights based on the excuse that they are two different genders. They attribute the physiological differences and physical characteristics of the two genders as the reasons for gender-based discrimination and inequality. They see men as strong and women as weak, men as rational and women as mentally deficient, men as managers and women as incapable, men as social, and women as passive.

The thoughts of the Mullahs have been one of the main factors in historical gender discrimination in Iran. Introducing women as the second and worthless gender had been promoted for hundreds of years by religious preachers. If they came to power with their rotten ideologies, it was obvious that they would restrict women in all aspects of their lives, and unfortunately, that's exactly what happened. The founder of the Islamic Republic, Ruhollah Khomeini, refers to granting women the right to vote and the permission to choose and be chosen as the starting point and the reason for his opposition to the previous monarchy.

In a speech against women's social activities, he says:

"See what you have done? You have allowed women into offices; look at any office they have entered, that office has become paralyzed. It is restricted; scholars forbid it. Do not send them to provinces. If a woman enters a system, she disrupts the situation."

This form of implementation of regressive laws in a political system pushed the people of Iran to the point of an explosive revolution against the Islamic regime's integrity decades later. The mistaken and completely wrong revolution of 1979 in Iran, which was created as a tragedy, with the influences of Muslim and Communist groups, had gotten tangled up with the leadership of an illiterate, ignorant, and anti-women Mullah. However, the genre and content of the "Woman, Life, Freedom" revolution and the current young and modern generation of Iran have no association with the anti-modern concepts, desires, and goals of the ideologies from 1979.

Iranians not only do not see tradition and religion as the source of laws, but they also consider them as interference in the country's laws as obstacles to progress and development. Accepting and embracing secularism is the meaning of such a viewpoint, which is one of the fundamental conditions for development. Mullahs have a fundamental conflict with such an approach. They consider managing the country and legislation with divine origin and criterion as the basis of society's progress.

They enforce and approve all the laws in the country based on Islamic Sharia's criteria.

If they pass anti-women and gender-based laws in the Islamic Consultative Assembly, it is to exert more control over the people, especially women.

I believe that anyone who removes Islamic religion and Sharia from their analysis of the crimes and behavior of the Islamic government is speaking in an unrealistic void because the basis of the discrimination and thoughts of Mullahs is derived from and inspired by Islamic Sharia. The argument that Mullahs' Islam in Iran is different from Mullahs' Islam in Saudi Arabia or that Egyptian Islam is different from Turkish Islam is an excuse to safeguard the intervention of Sharia in suppressing women. The control of women by Mullahs' laws has been happening for several hundred years now.

Suppression and suffocation have arisen from within Islamic culture, and the evidence for this statement is the lived experiences of humans under all religious governments and the historical record of suppressive Islamists and Islamic fundamentalists against women and nonconformists. If women have been suppressed in Iran, it has been through the laws of the Islamic government and the holy book as the criterion and basis. If a woman does not have the right to freedom of dress, if wearing a hijab is mandatory, or if there is gender discrimination between women and men, it is due to factors and causes, the most important one being the religious views of Mullahs and religious authorities.

When women, who make up half of society, are not recognized, and women's suppression is considered legal and normal, it is natural for Iran's modern and free generation to include women's rights among their main slogans. This is highlighting the historical oppression that women have endured. It gives us hope for a future that strives for gender equality and justice. They demand the elimination of discriminatory laws against women, which have become normalized and accepted. And they seek to dismantle the mindset that considers women as inferior and men as superior. This mindset seeks to confine and imprison women, keeping them hidden away from the public, in their homes.

In this path, any rational individual seeks the most efficient and least harmful route to achieve their goal. They only resort to a risky way when the current situation poses a greater threat than the risk of change.

If Iranian women have resorted to street protests against the Islamic regime, that's because they can't find any other way to get their message across and their rights respected. They consider the risk of fighting preferable to their current situation. Since continuing the current status is unacceptable to them, they have risked their lives, come onto the streets of Iran, and demonstrated such courage that shatters the false image portrayed by the regime and Mullahs. If someone describes his or her life in a few words, those words, despite their brevity, will reflect the most about their situation. If women's rights have become a fundamental principle and cornerstone of the "Woman, Life, Freedom" revolution for Iranians, it is a reflection of the women's situation within the laws and conditions created by the Mullahs' regime. Although, in many industrialized or developing countries, gender discrimination exists, the outcry and protests against it are not heard.

The fact that people in the heart of the Middle East are staging a revolution for women's status, gender equality, and freedom is a precious cultural gem that must be protected with all our might. This kind of revolution means breaking the stereotypes against Iranians.

In fact, it is an unparalleled revolution, which has a cultural content in the geography of the Middle East.

In how many countries (even modern ones) are men willing to get shot and stand against the most brutal government in support of women's rights? The fact that many Iranian men are wholeheartedly raising the banner of gender equality and sacrificing their lives on this path, advancing the revolution with widespread support for women, signifies nothing but freedom and sacrifice. That courage and resistance are inspiring and a symbol to other men around the world. They know that many Iranian men have given their lives to liberate women, who are forced to live by the regime's laws, and Iranian women have sacrificed themselves so as not to live in the captivity of tyrants. In fact, in the "Woman, Life, Freedom", revolution, the word 'human' has found meaning on the streets. Women and men stood side by side and sacrificed for each other's rights.

Here is a beautiful interpretation – when Gökay Akbulut, a representative in the German parliament, addresses the Iranian people, and says, *"You are a symbol of justice and democracy."*

Such interpretations have been repeated by Western politicians because Iranian revolutionaries were the true examples of these statements. Iranians introduced themselves in this way, while the Mullahs tried to show to the rest of the world, through Islamic hijab, that Iranian society is Islamic. In reality, women's bodies became a show to encourage people and Iranian society to be more religious. While Iranian women did not want to be supernumerary forces in the game of deception and falsehood of the Mullahs. They do not want to be a symbol of the religiosity of the country. That is why many women and girls removed the imposed hijab from their heads and set it on fire. This behavior meant the comprehensive disgust of women toward mandatory clothing. It meant expressing hatred against all forms of discrimination they experienced. This behavior also meant that women were saying a resounding *"NO!"* to the Islamic government, which has used hijab as a tool to control women and make it part of its regime's identity. Such acts were a departure from misogynistic traditions and a confrontation with patriarchal and religious manifestations. It meant becoming free from the shackles and constraints imposed on women from childhood. It was a declaration of women's rejection of imposed religion and traditions.

In developed countries, women hold the highest government, judicial, and national positions. They are decision-makers. But the Mullahs, as hostage takers, have deprived women of even managing their own lives. In the 21st century, an era witnessing much remarkable progress in all aspects, Iranian women do not have the right to divorce or get separated! They cannot even independently decide whether to continue or end their marital relationships.

In a time when Sanna Marin is the Prime Minister of Finland, Sophie Wilmès is the Prime Minister of Belgium, Mette Frederiksen is the Prime Minister of Denmark, Jacinda Ardern is the Prime Minister of New Zealand, and Kersti Kaljulaid is the President of Estonia, the Mullahs' regressive regime has taken away from Iranian women their rights to travel, divorce, and choose clothes freely.

The Mullahs' views lack an understanding of gender equality, the role of women, and their social presence. The Mullahs consider women as the cause of deceiving men and, therefore, consistently advise that women stay away from social gatherings and refrain from participating in society. Essentially, the conflict between Iranians and the Mullahs is a struggle between tradition and modernity. Tradition, which cannot comprehend modernity, has forced people to resort to a revolution. Even mutual understanding between them has become almost impossible. People say one thing, and the Mullahs understand the opposite. They interpret gender equality as social corruption, consider freedom of choice in clothing as pornography, interpret women's rights as the collapse of the family, and label the right to choose, at all, as depravity. In fact, the Mullahs have become so immersed in tradition and religion that they have lost the power of thinking.

Of course, some Mullahs, due to their disbelief in the Islamic foundations, are capable of understanding the rightful words of the people. However, since continuing their current situation is providing them with immense positions, income, and wealth, they intentionally ignore and deny the people's desires.

There is a fundamental rule that is highly important and worthy of attention, which is this: Humans have fundamental rights regardless of gender, orientation, or nationality. No government can take away or grant these fundamental rights to individuals. Governments are not in a position to deprive or grant these rights, but rather, individuals *inherently and automatically* possess these basic rights. There is no need for approval in parliaments or national assemblies.

As a human being, you are entitled to human rights. Governments are obligated only to create a safe and secure ground in legislative assemblies to facilitate the use of inherent rights by people. Gender equality is also part of human rights. Governments do not have the right to impose discrimination and inequality based on gender. When such rights are systematically violated by the government, it not only commits a crime against the country's population but also generates anger and social hatred toward the systems, to the extent that the accumulation of such events increases the probability of the collapse, at any moment, of a corrupt structure. The Iranian revolution also arose from the density and intensification of the violation of Iranians' natural and citizenship rights. If the quality and quantity of street protests by the Iranian people (especially women) was astonishing, it has a direct relationship with the discrimination and injustice imposed by the Islamic government. These social explosions' intensity corresponds to the level of suppression and restrictions.

In which part of the world women do not have the right to enter sports stadiums? Entering stadiums freely is not the most important need and right of women but preventing them from entering stadiums is a sign of the tremendous restrictions imposed on them. In the 21st century, Iranian women do not have permission to enter stadiums to watch sports competitions! It can be said confidently that there is no such level of brutality against women in any other country. The extent and form of oppression and suffocation that exist against women in Iran have disrupted their normal and natural lives, and this trend is considered ordinary and commonplace by some. Insane Mullahs believe that a divine and holy source has given them permission for such behavior, and these delusions solidify them in their wrong position and consider deviating from religious laws as a denial of God's word and religion.

Iranian women and men started their revolution with the goal of freedom – freedom from Mullahs, freedom from oppressive laws, freedom for women, and so on. Of course, society cannot progress without the freedom and independence of women.

A society with gender inequality is backward, even if it is full of towers and palaces. A society that does not consider women's rights and freedom to be important is regressive. Women's rights are important because humans are important. The historical oppression of women has reached its endpoint, and Iranians will bury discrimination, and misogyny in the history books with the "Woman, Life, Freedom" revolution.

If the voices and cries of free people have not been heard from the heart of the Middle East, it does not mean that such people do not exist. Rather, it signifies their suppression and censorship. In systems where there are long-term prison sentences and torture for the minimum social and political activities, it is clear that many engage in self-censorship. If others judge, based on their knowledge of the conditions of Middle Eastern governments, that there are no liberals and democrats in the Middle East, they have made an incorrect and unrealistic judgment. For decades, the Islamic government has imprisoned liberal individuals for even the slightest imaginable activity, with judicial orders. In such circumstances, some restrict and censor themselves, while others devotedly continue to fight. For example, the Islamic government has sentenced Saba Kurd Afshari, a girl who was walking without an Islamic hijab, to 24 years in prison, and Marzieh Yousefzadeh, a 26-year-old citizen from Mahabad, who was peacefully protesting alone with a placard that had Mahsa Amini's name written on it before the protests began, was arrested and sentenced to 15 years in prison. These numbers represent the years of life that a person has. Years that are now jeopardized for acting in accordance with their own rights.

These numbers are not just fleeting figures to be mentioned and forgotten. For each passing year of these numbers, the imprisoned hero of the Iranian nation waits 365 days to experience the outside world again and meet their friends, while gradually succumbing to mental degradation.

We are unaware of to what extent women had to endure all the insults and humiliations. How were they able to withstand any mistreatment and verbal abuse? All that strain and stress will result in the loss of the best years of their life and youth. Their minds will be consumed by daily pain that others cannot comprehend, while others will remain unaware of their feelings and homesickness. They will be lonely and trapped in their homeland, confined to a corner. Such an occurrence inflicts a kind of double torment on the people who want freedom and democracy, via their hearts. By witnessing such events (imprisonment, torture, and execution), they endure indescribable suffering and grief for their dearest friends and comrades.

Such events are the result of the struggle against the terrorist Islamic regime … against a Mullah who utilizes crimes for his own purposes and has even employed sexual torture as a means of fighting and increasing fear.

It violates all moral and international laws simultaneously. Mullahs employ psychological warfare, which includes sexual assault as part of their techniques and operations, against the Iranian people. This is similar to the invading Russians, who utilized such methods in the war in Ukraine with aggression and brutality to defeat the Ukrainians and break their psychological resilience, which finally led to their humiliation and discredit. The Ukrainians' belief in their own values shattered the Russians and made them retreat. The Islamic government has also chosen such methods as a means of repression and psychological warfare. For example, they subjected Iranian hero Armita Abbasi, a 22-year-old woman, who was arrested during street protests, to sexual assault, and, within 24 hours of transferring her to the hospital, before her family could meet her, they moved her to an unknown location. CNN has thoroughly examined various published documents that have confirmed that the Islamic government uses sexual torture as a tool for psychological terror against democracy advocates.

This research report mentioned that many sexual torture acts were filmed to prevent the victims from speaking out against the regime and the atrocities that have occurred.

The Islamic regime's brutality and depravity led them to respond to the demand for gender equality by employing sexual torture as a tool. This is the stark reality of the Mullahs and the terrorist Revolutionary Guards (Sepah), who tried to hide it with lots of tricks. The guards sexually harass the girls and children of the land because they want freedom. This manner is exactly what we expected from the essence and nature of the Mullahs and the Sepah. Using this method, in addition to creating fear and terror among the Iranian people, they aim to carry out psychological warfare and break their spirit of resistance.

This behavior is one of the most blatant manifestations of the savagery of the Mullahs. The rape of women is evidence of the deep contradiction between the Iranian people uprising and the Islamic regime values. In fact, this behavior is a warning from the Islamic regime to other revolutionary women fighting that, if they are arrested, they will be subject to torture. It is a way to instill fear into the minds of the revolutionaries to weaken their motivation to fight, to destroy or break down their fighting capability. Their goal is to create rumination in the minds of the revolutionary individuals, so they think, *"What if I get arrested and am subjected to torture? What if I, who detests oppressors, become a victim of their sexual harassment?"* And these continuous questions going through their minds can ultimately lead to discouragement, fear, and weakening in some individuals.

This method of the Mullahs' government is a true example of terrorism. Creating organized fear and terror through the illegitimate suppression of the people is the most prominent form of government terrorism. However, the important point is that the people have the determining role in dealing with someone who has faced sexual torture. They are the heroes of the country because when someone is killed, they become a national hero, or the wounded person becomes a symbol of freedom and courage in the Iranian nation. Also, the person who has been sexually harassed should not be seen any differently by the people. The person who has been subjected to assault and harassment has paid the price of freedom with their body and soul and is now a national hero and symbol of courage. They are the legend and soul of Iranians. They are the purest embodiment of freedom and liberty. Gender-biased and traditional perspectives on the issue of sexual assault always exclude or isolate the victim, even before the onslaught of hurtful thoughts, which causes more psychological stress for them.

The impact of sexual harassment on society depends on the level of gender-biased culture within that society. If sexual relations are considered forbidden, then the government's use of sexual torture as a tool for public intimidation or excessive psychological harm to the victim would be more effective. The regime found it easier to control a gender-biased society. However, there is also a reverse consequence for the Mullahs as people will become more resolute and steadfast in their opposition to the regime. Any crime can double the motivation to fight and discredit the regime on a global scale. The regime's true nature will be exposed in front of the eyes of nations and governments. So, gender-biased perspectives and customs not only have negative effects on daily life but are also a tool that the Mullahs use in their psychological warfare against Iranians. A progressive and modern culture will disarm the Mullahs.

To defend the dignity and freedom of women, the revolution aims to eliminate gender-biased views and eradicate such erroneous perceptions. In an environment where half the population – women – are held captive by a patriarchal and religious system, growth and development will be an illusion. Such a system considers women's individuality to be the main enemy of the government's ideals. Before representing social roles, women are independent individuals. Being a woman does not solely define her as a daughter, sister, mother, or wife. A woman is an individual. She is herself. Social labels that disregard women's individuality are effective factors in creating various forms of discrimination. In other words, the Islamic government views and defines women as subordinates to other family members. Placing individuals within predetermined frameworks and imposing specific, unchosen duties are nothing but the suppression of women's individuality. In such conditions, the possibility of personal and social growth for women will be lost. Maternal and marital duties are defined in a way that hinder their personal growth.

Neither fathers nor husbands nor brothers have the right to violate the privacy and independence of women. They have no right to restrict women based on their gender. Women can live their own lives however they want and not as their fathers or families dictate. If there is a legitimate legal restriction, it should apply to everyone, and if there is freedom, it should be for everyone.

Also, human development indexes include both women and men. It is up to women whether they want to become a better version of themselves. They have the opportunity to discover and pursue their own goals and capabilities, not others. Governments are also obligated to support their citizens in this path. However, there is no doubt that the Islamic regime occupying Iran is against the growth of any individualism, especially the growth of women who oppose the regime.

Mullahs fail to understand that there is no inherent difference between Iranian women and American or European women. If, due to a coincidence or some kind of incident or event, a girl is born in Iran and falls under the control and captivity of the Islamic government, while another girl is born in a developed country and does not experience repression, none of these scenarios imply a difference in their needs. Rather, the difference lies in the structures that support one with liberal values and oppress the other with religious and traditional values.

If a plant does not grow properly, the issue is not within the plant itself but within the unfavorable environment and conditions, which have hindered the plant's potential growth. The soil, water, light, air, etc. should be examined, and a balance should be considered. In such conditions, growth is inevitable.

Iranians began a revolution to eliminate the obstacles to growth and development and to create conditions where they could freely pursue their life goals. Humans get only one opportunity and chance to experience life in the world, so they do not want to be mere extraneous forces in a mad dictator's game. They don't want to suffer at the hands of criminals, who have turned the people's chance to experience the world and feel freedom into such endless suffering.

Mullahs employ various methods to create such oppression and control. One of the methods they use (apart from using weapons) to enslave human lives is to control their minds.

In this regard, they use women to control society. In the Mullahs' view, the goal of a woman's life is motherhood, and a mother is responsible for raising her children. They believe that if women's thoughts are controlled and shaped according to their desires, their children will automatically become like their mothers. They believe that, instead of spending a lot of money to convince adults to lean toward Islamism, it is enough to control mothers so that their children are controlled unconsciously. In other words, using a beloved title, *mother*, to control a large part of society and confine them to within the boundaries of motherhood, while being a woman, is not equal to being a mother. If a woman decides not to be a mother, it is her decision, and she will not lose her worth. Motherhood is an extraordinary and unique characteristic, but it does not mean ideological exploitation of children. Essentially, even mothers don't have the right to impose such things. But Islamism and religious fanaticism have trapped the Mullahs in a crazy snare that permits such behaviors and considers them normal. This is how they control the next generation.

Another method that the Mullahs use to control and intimidate the Iranian nation is to fight against the meanings and ideals of their revolution. They introduce the slogans and demands of the people, especially women, through their own distorted and frozen understanding by manipulating the meanings. They interpret the people's "Woman, Life, Freedom" uprising as

nudity and uncontrolled sexual relationships to display a superficial concept of the disregarded rights of the Iranian people.

The first point is that the Mullahs are not able to have a correct understanding and logical comprehension of the demands
of the Iranian people. Their gender-biased mentality, Islamic
ideological thinking, and one-dimensional and ideological view
of the world will only always provide a suitable ground for the
growth of their prejudice and ignorance. The capacity of the mind
and the ability to understand are subject to various factors; not
everyone is capable of comprehending any subject. For example,
it would be a mere fantasy to talk about the problems of global
warming and environmental consequences with someone who
does not understand the most basic problems in their small society and expects them to understand. Also, talking to a young
child about quantum physics and Heisenberg's uncertainty principle and expecting them to comprehend such a subject is a big
mistake on our part. Due to the narrow views of the Mullahs,
who have dedicated their lives to promoting unjustifiable beliefs and a biased mentality, have formed in their views, they
lack the ability and capacity to understand the concepts of other
subjects. Therefore, understanding the "Woman, Life, Freedom"
slogan is beyond their cognitive and perceptual abilities.

The second point is that the Mullahs do not want the desired concepts of the revolution to grow and expand through
Iranian fighters. This is because, at the very least, they know
that the "Woman, Life, Freedom" revolution's perspective is a
stance against, and opposition to, the Islamic regime. In fact,
they likely see that everything they believed in and preached
is being denied. The system's ideology is experiencing collapse
and destruction at the societal level so they try to weaken and
undermine the ideals and values of the opposition front, making the revolutionaries appear weak and meaningless.

Such a method is one of the Mullahs' psychological warfare
tactics. However, methods that contain lies and deception will
not achieve the desired result. A method that denies the truth
and tells lies to reach its goal will not lead anywhere.

The Mullahs' behavior is like this: In a conversation that is taking place, one of the parties begins to attack the real character of the speaker to hide their weak logic. Such an attack is not for the sake of exposing the truth, but rather to deflect the negotiation from a specific topic and to obscure the conversation with irrelevant issues. The Mullahs want to offset their wrong thoughts and weak logic through evasion, distortion, and spreading lies. Of course, such a method will not benefit them, but it will be more proof of their depravity and their minds' corruption.

The logic of gender discrimination and the anti-human belief system has no solution other than displaying that the logic of its opponents is superficial.

The third point is that the concept of women's bodies in Islamic culture is taboo and a tool for Mullahs' policies. In fact, when the freedom of choice in clothing is allowed, Mullahs can no longer use women's bodies for their religious and political purposes. Based on the perspectives of Mullahs, women should be an army for Islamism. If women do not comply with such a duty and role, then the ideological power of the Mullahs will reach its end. They introduce women in veils as soldiers of their own ideology. They consider the veils and thick coverings of women to be a sign of endorsement and the strengthening of Islamism. In fact, by the presence of free, independent, and secular women, these kinds of abuses will end soon. Free clothing implies the destruction of the unreal authority and power of the regime by demonstrating an Islamic picture of society.

The fourth point is that Mullahs have always lived within their limitations, and they have had numerous constraints and social and behavioral boundaries in their lives. Many of them consciously and unconsciously carry complex resentment about the relationship between men and women. They confine themselves to the perspective of religious law and cannot tolerate others having the freedom to establish satisfying and better relationships. The fact that Mullahs and their followers are confined to the boundaries of religion leads them to envy and sorrow, which is reflected in their aggressive and anti-women behaviors.

Mullahs want to restrict everyone. Their mindset is that if we are limited by religious rules, then everyone in society should be limited as well. If I cannot live freely according to my beliefs, then others also do not have the right to live freely.

When they shape society according to their own beliefs, they experience joy and satisfaction. It is natural for such crazy individuals to interpret the avant-garde "Woman, Life, Freedom" slogan based on their personal life complexes. A life accompanied by depression and restrictions has made Mullahs, who consider it their undeniable right to interfere in human relationships, turn into evil creatures.

The fifth point is that nudity is a subject that the Islamic regime has chosen with which to interpret the subject of the people having the freedom to choose their clothing. Mullahs have confiscated Islamic clothing to the desired and display it as the Islamic nature of the country, even though types of clothing, including the hijab of some Muslim women in the country, do not mean the majority of the nation is Islamist. They interpret the freedom of clothing which is derived from the human right to one's own body, as nudity.

The choice of clothing is up to individuals, not governments. A society's citizens determine the shape and form of their clothes. Religion, tradition, and government have no right to determine people's attire. The opinions of others also have no validity in choosing the clothing style of others. *If someone's idea about my type of clothing is binding, then my opinion about their type of clothing will also be binding for sure.*

If someone believes that Islamic hijab or covering the body is right, then someone else can believe nudity is right. As a result, we will have thousands of different binding standards that are impractical and considered a violation of others' privacy. Freedom of clothing means freedom of any clothing, not prescribing a specific version.

Is it not possible for some people to wear revealing clothes and disrupt societal norms? Yes, it is possible, but the choice of open or short clothing is their right. If a part of society wants to wear short or revealing clothes, that has nothing to do with anyone. If the behavior of assault becomes normalized, interfering in people's lives will also seem normal. In many developed countries, there is not even a binding law to enforce wearing a minimum of clothing, let alone a specific kind of clothing.

In a typical society, people choose their clothes based on their own considerations and choices. The freedom to choose their own clothing means citizens have the freedom to cover or not cover their bodies, encompassing the various kinds of clothing. Of course, Mullahs who have never heard anything except the whisper of coercion in their ears will not understand the concept of having options and human preferences.

The sixth point is that what the Mullahs consider to be corruption is actually a reflection of their own perspective, not the people's. They consider it corrupt for women to be free in their clothing. Their interpretation, of course, differs from the interpretation of others. They even perceive the visible and uncovered hair of women as a cause of social corruption and the destruction of ethics and family, whereas their moral and social standards are derived from vague historical religion and religious traditions.

They consider sexual relations between a man and woman, outside of marriage, as corruption, when these relationships are not corrupt at all. Rather, they are necessary and among the most natural inclinations of human beings. The standards of ethics and truth differ greatly between the Mullahs and Iranian citizens.

What is the basis for corruption? For Mullahs, Islamic law and sectarian interests determine corruption and its instances. For example, if we talk about the freedom of expression and ask why Shiite clerics have the right to freely express their opinions in promoting Sharia and politics in Iran, but their opponents do not have such rights and privileges; their answer is, *"The ideas of the opponents will cause misguidance and corruption of society"*. That is the answer I received when I had a conversation with one of the present Shia Mullahs (One of the authorities on matters of religion), Javadi Amoli. Freedom of expression, which is an undeniable right, is turned into a subject of corruption. In fact, corruption is a perpetual concept and arena, used against anything that weakens their position and status.

With this kind of understanding of corruption, any behavior conflicting with religious thinking will be considered corrupt. Such patients fundamentally lack the right to define the concept and instances of corruption, which is why the Iranian people fundamentally deny the standards of the Islamic government in an unprecedented manner. Iranians do not measure corruption standards with religious indicators. Corruption standards in any field are not based on tradition, Mullahs, or religion. Iranians shout for a revolution whose foundation and essence is rationality. Modern humans make decisions with their own values in mind, based on collective and individual wisdom.

There is a need for extensive evidence and documentation that can be objectively verified and logically argued, to determine what action causes corruption, or *what* is corrupt. When a Mullah closes his eyes and opens his mouth – while relying on shallow and empty arguments from a few historical books – labels modern human life as corrupt, it stems from their delusional and self-righteous ideological thinking.

The three concepts used in the Iranian Revolution's slogan, which is "Woman, Life, Freedom", are interrelated. These three concepts are not separate from each other; each word has a direct connection to the others. Life without freedom is meaningless, just as freedom without respecting women's rights is not true freedom. Life without equality among people becomes as empty as freedom separated from a desirable life. In each of these concepts, the other clearly plays its role. Freedom is for all people in society, not for a specific gender. It is for all the people in the country, not for a particular ideology. When we talk about freedom, it includes everyone without discrimination and inequality.

It is evident that, in Iran, neither men nor women nor other genders, have had any share of freedom. However, even with the lack of freedom, they have not been equal to each other. Some have experienced more severe restrictions. The conditions and limitations facing the LGBTQ community cannot be described with any words or phrases. They have experienced the most challenging restrictions and constraints possible. The women of Iranian society have long been the main target of discrimination and censorship, and they are still a target. They have experienced more limitations and suffocation than men. Some prisoners (Iranian people), experiencing horrible conditions and have even more restrictions. Destroying and renovating this vast prison, which has been turned into an unbearable hell at the hands of the Mullahs, is the revolution's main goal and clear path.

Assuming there is no freedom, the possibility of any form of injustice and corruption occurring exists because the individuals who will fight against corruption will not be free to take action. Injustices will continue to flourish, and no one will have the right to prevent them.

This is why Karl Popper, a thoughtful liberal philosopher, has said:

"If I have to choose between justice and freedom, I choose freedom because, in a free but unjust society, I have the freedom to defend justice. But in a society that has taken away my freedom in the name of justice, if justice is not achieved, I don't even have the freedom to protest."

Human beings are born free, and freedom is among their fundamental rights. If it is not enforced in some countries, it does not mean that people do not have such a right. Rather, it means that there are conditions that hinder the exercise of their fundamental human right. Governments are obligated to create ways for humans to act freely. States are established to manage society in a way that the freedoms of citizens do not unnecessarily interfere with each other. But rather, there should be a mechanism where more citizens can exercise their freedom and be less restricted.

If governments were to eradicate all humans' freedom, then the institution that was created to enforce and protect fundamental freedoms would become its opposite. In such a situation, citizens have the right to remove the obstacle from their path in any way proportionate to the situation because freedom is not negotiable. Without freedom, human life is propelled toward absurdity, talents are destroyed, and people become hopeless. Human beings can't be themselves without freedom, rather they are others. Without freedom, we are not ourselves. Imposed appearances and behaviors do not represent us. They represent the person, agency, or government that imposed those thoughts and tastes upon us. The existence of freedom allows us to manifest our true personality and preferences.

Without freedom, we would find ourselves in a black hole where everything is dark and terrifying. But the expression and implementation of human views and desires will bring them peace and satisfaction. That is why the level of happiness and life satisfaction in developed and democratic countries is significantly higher than in authoritarian countries. If citizens of Scandinavian countries are consistently known to have the happiest societies, it is the result of mechanisms that eliminate oppression and governmental control. Also, those societies provide conditions for the expression of one's thoughts, enthusiasm, and art. If we compare an individual's feeling when they are in prison to their feeling of happiness when they are released from prison, we can better understand the impact of freedom on living a joyful life.

The level of freedom is directly related to the level of happiness. A free society will be a happy society. Freedom affects everything, making everything more vibrant and transparent, from our behavior to the governance of a country. Dictators, aware of the benefits of freedom, seek to eliminate freedom because they do not want a happy and transparent society. Freedom provides the foundation for transparency, and transparency is the factor that leads to the downfall of dictators. The concept of freedom in the revolution's slogan pertains to all types of freedom, from individual freedoms to political and economic freedoms. From freedom of government interventions to interventions of a specific group in society through religious privileges which allows dictators to interfere in the lives of others.

Authoritarian institutions and governments intentionally erase citizens' rightful freedoms to create a space for their oppressive presence. They control society through their interventions in public and private spheres. Dictators know that more free citizens mean a more limited government. The greater the penetration of governments into society, the less freedom and more suffocation there will be.

Society does not need a maximal government, but it needs maximum freedom. Dictators pursue their own ambitions by forming extensive governments; usually, big governments mean less freedom and more corruption.

One of the goals of advanced democracies is to reduce government interference and increase freedom. Excessive government authority signifies setting maximum limits and boundaries, whereas minimal government powers would allow healthy competition to happen among people's ideas and businesses. Many may consider government intervention in various aspects of people's lives as benevolent interference when, in fact, a great evil arises from the consolidation of all possible powers in one institution. When the economy, culture, education, military forces, administrative systems, etc. are all under the influence and control of governments, then, without a doubt, competition and any flourishing will be destroyed.

Democratic citizens generate their own relevant institutions in society; this is similar to how it is in developed countries, where people create the economy and social infrastructure. It is through people's competition that different arenas of the country are managed. The government's role, if necessary, would be the regulator of relationships.

Giving excessive power to the government and excluding citizens from managing society ultimately leads to uncontrollable and terrifying suffocation. A government that possesses weapons, suppresses, controls the economy, threatens protesters, controls politics, and eliminates opponents does not result in happy citizens. A government that interferes in the private lives of citizens and is not accountable will bring about only the destruction of citizens' lives. Such tragedies have befallen and continue to happen in many societies because their governments and authorities have extensive, large, and uncontrollable powers. If governments are small, they do not possess the economy, they are not allowed to intervene in the lives of citizens, and they cannot use the economy and military tools as ways to suppress the people.

In such a situation, the citizen is the absolute power, not the government. Citizens and their resources support the government, not anything else. In such a scenario, if the government tends to lean toward dictatorship, it can be controlled and overthrown through the free flow of information, the freedom of the press, and political actions. The downfall of certain governments that lean toward autocracy is indebted to preexisting freedom. This previously existing freedom prevents suffocation before it occurs. Therefore, dictators restrict citizens' freedoms through laws and their interference to avoid downfall.

The occupying Islamic regime in Iran has also been aware of that. It believes in maximum government control and has created a large bureaucratic system. It has attempted to deprive its citizens of even a minimal amount of freedom so as not to provide any opening for change and transformation.

In other words, the Islamic regime has destroyed political and economic competition and eradicated individuals' freedoms through government interference. When all aspects of people's lives are under the control of a totalitarian government, the slogan of *freedom* naturally takes on a profound difference. In this situation, the word freedom encompasses all dimensions of life, from personal lifestyles to political competition. Of course, the prerequisite for such freedoms is liberation from the corruption that is the Islamic government. Since the Islamic government cannot implement democracy and freedom, the slogan of freedom from the people means the removal and downfall of the regime.

The people's concept of freedom is not the twisted and distorted interpretation among the Mullahs, trivialize and misinterpret freedom, just like their portrayal of the slogan *woman*. The Mullahs' ideological mindset perceives freedom as being unrestrained or a lack of commitment, whereas freedom means the power of choice and a voluntary and conscious commitment to something.

A person who is not free is not truly committed. Living the kind of life that exists forcibly and imposed will never amount to anything other than people's self-alienation. The Mullahs interpret freedom as being without restrictions, but in reality, restrictions refer to limitations and commitments. But Mullahs cannot recognize limitations or have the right to determine commitments. Behavioral boundaries and adherence to commitments have a proviso, which is freedom. Limitations and commitments are meaningless without freedom. Limitation means being free to act but only up to a specific boundary. Having limitations does not mean infinite and endless boundaries. Freedom gives meaning to limitations, while limitations cannot define freedom.

How do Islamists, who have no understanding of freedom, determine the boundaries of freedom? How do the Mullahs, who only deal with God and religion, talk about commitments between humans? Those who do not consider themselves accountable to the people and claim to derive their legitimacy from God will not have any commitment to the Iranian people.

They do not see the government as a structure that arises from the will of the people, which should be committed to respecting and fulfilling the rights of the people. They see control over people and natural resources in the country as an opportunity to expand and enforce Islam. They have put all of Iran's potential at the service of Islam and their own close groups. There is no commitment between them and the Iranian people.

The result of the Mullahs' domination has appeared in the form of religious and political boundaries and limitations, which interfere in and control even the most private matters of people, such as their clothing. They introduce such interventions as religious restrictions and also use the phrase *religious obligations and commitments*, which they mentioned when they came to power, saying that the determination of the ruler will be one of people's rights.

This is the famous statement of the founder of the Islamic regime, Ruhollah Khomeini, in which he expressed how he was against the previous monarchy government:

"Even if the Shah of Iran serves the people and works toward their welfare, if the people do not want him, he must go."

But the Mullahs and religious leaders showed their commitment by brutally suppressing Iranian children in front of the eyes of the nations and governments of the world in action. With their war weapons, they killed Iranian men and women who protested, and they didn't even allow their families to hold funeral ceremonies. (These are the *boundaries and restrictions* and *burdens and commitments* of the Mullahs and religious leaders). Therefore, the most unrestrained moving creatures – I mean the Mullahs and religious leaders – have no right to interpret the noble and glorious concept of freedom.

They distort beautiful and meaningful concepts by the absurd management and governance they display. They turned a wealthy country into one of the most devastated and inefficient countries with policies that are so wrong. Any action this group takes leads to nothing but destruction. Instead of reciting eulogies and prayers over graves, the Mullahs have become decision-makers for a pioneering nation and historical country.

Their habits and methods are to take away the meanings of words so they can portray their opponent's intentions as empty. The point is that, without limitations and commitments, it is natural for people to engage in some wrong behavior while being unrestrained, which is the Mullahs' intent and is part of the fundamental basic and citizenship rights of people. Their definition of words does not resonate with the conventional understanding of humans. For example, a Mullah might consider the lack of commitment to the guardianship of the jurist as being unrestrained while, from the perspective of an Iranian, not being committed to the institution of the guardianship of the jurist is one of their fundamental demands! A modern person may consider polygamy as being unrestrained, but the Mullahs consider polygamy to be among the legitimate religious and legal rights of men. Therefore, the interpretation of freedom as being without restrictions is a ridiculous distortion. Essentially, there is no possibility of a common definition of freedom between the rulers and the people of Iran.

Accurate definitions of overriding concepts are crucial because they directly relate to the lives of human beings. Without a clear and precise definition of these concepts, some may be inclined toward deceivers, such as the Mullahs and authoritarian politicians. In fact, all *rights and freedoms* and *various forms and contents of governments* are designed for one purpose, which is the welfare and security of humans. A political system that does not fulfill its main mission and duty and pursues a goal other than well-being, security, and people's rights is illegitimate and discredited. The concept of *life*, which is also one of the three main slogans of the revolution, refers to the purpose of forming governments. The authentic concept of freedom serves the concept of life. The concept of gender equality does not refer to anything other than a better life. But some, for various reasons, such as religion, personal ambitions, and ideological distortions, have gambled with people's lives when it concerns their false mentalities.

In this situation, the concept of *life* loses meaning and becomes worthless repetitive living. In fact, life is not just breathing, growing, reproducing, and conforming. It is being alive, which is a profound difference from life. Being alive is an opportunity for living. A person who commits suicide does not find their own existence meaningful due to the lack of a desirable flow of life. Dictators also take away people's lives and even demand that people stay alive to serve them.

Mullahs and clerics may also consider life as a specific way of living, but the purpose of life for them is different from the purpose of life for a normal human being. Mullahs seek to sacrifice people's lives for ideological goals. The fundamental difference between Iranians and Mullahs is this issue. Here is an example: An Iranian sees life as pursuing their own desires within a suitable framework and with the goal of happiness and joy, but the rulers of the Islamic government consider people having a happy and full life as a temporary path in which any event or form of living will not matter in terms of religious and ideological goals.

They kill others and are willing to die, themselves, for the sake of living in a world other than humans' material world. They restrict the lives of others to obtain rewards from immaterial beings. Unfortunately, this unbelievable event has become an entangling reality in the present era. In this situation, there is no common ground that enables mutual understanding. They have taken something as a criterion, that cannot be tested, for truth, examined, or measured. Something based on personal faith and belief. However, the basis of a rational human's decision-making is measurement, presenting results, and assessing the consequences of said decision. In this situation, the logic of the two opposing sides appears irrational and contradictory to each other. But who pays the cost of this disagreement between the Mullahs and Iranians? Iranian citizens will pay the cost with their lives, wealth, and future, and this is unacceptable. It makes no sense for the people of Iran to pay the price for the Mullahs' views, to which they are fundamentally opposed; this has no meaning except as an invasion and exploitation of the lives of others by the Mullahs.

The Islamic government leader's insane goal is to create an Islamic society. In this process and his view, if the lives of Iranians are destroyed, then that is a requirement for the realization of the Islamic government; they have repeatedly expressed this idea and perspective. They interpret the destruction of the lives of Iranians as problems that are normal and prevalent in all countries. In other words, it doesn't matter if the Iranians' wealth and efforts are destroyed – it doesn't matter that the nation is dissatisfied. The destruction of the hopes and future of children and youth is not important because some people want the Islamic government's expansion and consolidation as well as their own interests.

They consider themselves accountable to God, not to the people. Therefore, everything should be in line with pleasing God and serving Islamism. However, of course, another group has taken the path of betraying the Iranian nation with a deceptive approach and without belief in the Islamic religion or government.

The following statement that the chief advisor to the regime's Supreme Leader, Ali Akbar Velayati, said clearly reflects the extent of their disregard for the lives of Iranians: *"Let's learn resistance from the Yemenis. Instead of wearing clothes, they wear bath-covering cloth and eat dry bread."*

The roots of corruption and delusion propose Yemeni-style life and adopting the militia lifestyle of the Houthi forces to Iranian modernists! If the destruction of Iranians' lives, while on the path of fighting against other countries, is a potential issue, it isn't. Instead, according to Velayati, they should be content with dry bread and bath coverings, like some Yemenis, so that a bunch of psychotics can expand the Islamic government, and the ruling thieves can continue their criminal activities. This way of life has absolutely no connection to what the Iranians want or to their preferred way of life. It is horrific how people in the present era turn into creatures to pursue personal goals and engage in such dangerous games with their congener lives!

Due to two very contradictory interpretations of the concept of life between Iranians and Mullahs, each represents a different path in politics.

If Iranians' national assets are handed over to the proxy forces and militia armed groups by a terrorist, Ali Khamenei, and his subordinate groups, there is no reason for that to happen other than he considers the Iranians to be unimportant in his Islamic ideological thoughts. If Khamenei and his groups were to relocate to a desert and try to create a better afterlife world for themselves, away from society and people, then the cost of such actions would be with themselves. Taking a country's citizens and a nation's assets hostage, seizing the country's resources without the consent of its people, and simultaneously seeking to expand their desired ideology equates to nothing but depravity and the shameless plundering of others' wealth and possessions. The wealth that could have been used to provide housing, welfare, educational systems, and infrastructure development in the country is, instead, being spent on others whose affiliations or inclinations are not related to Iran and the Iranians.

When Iranians speak about *life*, they mean the country's potential should be used for their well-being and should not be used for the sake of the welfare of others who are the cause and agent of their own country's destruction. There is no common ground between Iranians and quasi-military groups, such as Hezbollah in Lebanon, the Houthis in Yemen, and the Popular Mobilization Forces in Iraq (al Hashd al-Shaabi). But in fact, Iranians are disgusted by their ideas and hate them. These groups are striving to establish governments similar to the Islamic regime in their own countries, and the Mullahs are providing them with the necessary equipment as well as financial and military support through theft and embezzlement.

In a world that is advancing and developing rapidly, Iranians have been afflicted with psychotics, which have led to the destruction of normal and conventional life in various arenas. Mullahs, who only understand life as building missiles to ensure their own security, interpret all aspects of life in a one-dimensional and security-oriented manner. They fail to understand that life is a comprehensive concept with various dimensions and aspects. In reality, to have a desirable life, there must be a suitable environment, which the Mullahs have not hesitated to destroy.

A prosperous life requires a powerful, productive, and free economy, which the Mullahs have not established, as they have done nothing of the sort except engage in raw-material exports and nationalize all resources. The prerequisite for a desirable life is an effective and efficient educational system, which, in all dimensions, from ideological textbooks to dissatisfied teachers and professors, are affected by these awful decisions. Under such circumstances, Iranians find their own lives in a state of ruin after 44 years of the Islamic regime; therefore, they consider restoring the authentic concept and embodiment of *life* as part of the progressive principles of the "Woman, Life, Freedom" revolution.

While many parts of Iran are witnessing widespread and unimaginable deprivation, and although, after the Islamic government was established, there has been over a trillion dollars of oil exported, we are witnessing extensive backwardness throughout the country. Some countries request loans of several million dollars from the International Monetary Fund, while the ignorant Mullahs fail to understand the value of the country's assets, opportunities, and free resources. They are only bringing about the benefit of oligarchs and the major thieves of the government.

Some countries lack natural resources but are prosperous, while others are rich in land and natural resources but poor. The reason for the existence of wealth and poverty is tied to the way of managing and planning the country. The existence of natural resources, which is a national privilege compared to other countries, has not been used for the benefit of the Iranian people and they have become a catastrophe for the country's economy, which is relying on oil and raw material exports. From this path, the traitor Mullahs also feel a sense of independence from the people. These Mullahs have turned the unique advantage of Iran into a threat, an economic-paralyzing factor, and a tool for internal repression.

The Mullahs have abandoned profitable industries and turned toward raw material exports, which means that they have no understanding of processing, added value, employment, and sustainable economy. They have managed the country's economic structure in a way, that, in the absence of oil and gas, the great country of Iran will be greatly paralyzed and impoverished in an instant. Investments and industries, like tourism, banking, telecommunications, automotive, information technology, and electronics, are considered global money-making industries, but the Islamic government has done nothing but sell crude oil and minerals to make quick income and inject capital into military industries and quasi-military forces.

The Mullahs claimed that if they came to power, they would transform people's lives to the extent that would even elevate people's spirituality. But the ignorant Mullahs fail to understand that achieving a desirable life without providing the necessary prerequisites for such a goal in a planned manner is just empty talk and baseless promises.

Presenting slogans that are deceitful and empty in content and highlighting grand claims and small achievements is the result of the unrealistic mindset of the Mullahs. The reality of the world is not determined by slogans and words but by specific principles and methods. In despotic systems, it is claimed that they will achieve the highest levels of welfare and security, but they never do because lies and exaggerations do not create reality. And the world's reality does not await our words, desires, and tastes. They speak of an excellent and prosperous life, but they have neither a correct understanding of such a life nor any thoughts to create the foundation or conditions for it.

Without a doubt, creating conditions that pave the way for a desirable life in society requires knowledge, expertise, and patriotism. The Mullahs and clerics have no competence or capacity in this regard, and relying on traditions, the Quran, and Islamic jurisprudence cannot govern a whole country. Mullahs cannot comprehend the importance of national responsibility. Their ideological fanaticism hinders understanding the catastrophic damage and loss they inflict on the country.

Therefore, the slogan *life* means removing the Mullahs from the position of managing the country and replacing them with capable and deserving individuals. Removing obstacles is a prerequisite for achieving a goal. The Islamic government hinders the creation of suitable conditions for a desirable life. With this description, the first stage of Iranian success is nothing but the removal of the Islamic regime and the elimination of the main factor of backwardness, and the next stage would be the establishment of a suitable and efficient alternative system. A productive economy, culture, and rights are the foundations of life. Life emerges from the accumulation of suitable conditions. Different components of the prerequisites of life put together create the whole called a desirable life.

With a weak economy, extremist culture, and the absence of individual and social rights, life will automatically disappear. It is not a matter of bullying and claiming; it is a reality that follows natural principles. If the foundations are not established yet, there will be no desirable life.

A weak economic structure leads to widespread poverty. And poverty becomes a barrier to many successes and the cause of many failures. The reduction in purchasing power, the depreciation of money, and extremely low incomes make people disheartened and hopeless about their goals, and such a state is against a good life. A citizen who lacks financial ability cannot manage their own affairs, and these inabilities mean the destruction of their inner aspirations, psychological damage, and suppressed desires. The ongoing effort to provide the minimum necessities of life has no meaning other than the erosion and destruction of individual goals and hopes.

Regular citizens don't have the opportunity to think about their personal growth. These citizens can't live the way they desire and are trapped in the middle of financial problems. Therefore, the slogan *life* directly refers to one of the determining factors, which is the citizen's economic power and the level of expenses and income. Meanwhile, on the contrary, the Mullahs have caused the currency (Rial) to be the most worthless money in the world with their recklessness and have caused the foundation of the government economy to be based on Rent (Economic Rent) and full of corruption and inflation, which has disintegrated society with no positive outcome.

Mullahs have destroyed lives and indifferently defer the responsibility for these events to their enemies. Parents have become ashamed of their children, teenagers yearn for conventional and simple possessions, and young people are submerged in financial problems and unable to provide the initial conditions for starting a family. Mullahs do not accept responsibility for any of their managed achievements! (or failures), while they are still shameless and act with unprecedented audacity.

Government officials in developed and democratic countries manage prosperous nations without a sense of superiority or bullying, where citizens can pursue their desired lives with minimal expenses. However, the corrupt and incompetent Mullahs, with a record of mismanaging national wealth, have set the fire of ignorance and foolishness, destroying every opportunity. Yet, they still claim superiority and pretend to promote ethics and morality. They remain silent on matters related to governments but exert all their power on issues unrelated to governance.

Essentially, the meaning and spirituality in citizens' lives have no connection to governments and ruling regimes. Such matters are related to the individuals' perspectives about the world. A government's responsibility lies solely in promoting welfare, security, and advocating for rights. The fact that they forget about people's welfare, security, and rights and, instead, strive to create a specific spirituality is wrong, harmful, and pointless. Because the purpose of forming a government will be forgotten, and spirituality becomes a tool for corruption and oppression. The involvement of governments in spirituality is harmful and creates a one-dimensional and unidirectional perspective, laying the foundation for social discrimination and gaps.

With this description, the desire and slogan of *life* are contradictory to the factors that hinder a desirable life. It opposes the destructive ideas of Mullahs. Life's slogan is against death, while the Mullahs bring death and destruction. They scare human beings with death and guide them toward death, but this revolution with a desire for life and freedom conflicts with that.

IRANIANS' REVOLUTION AND ISLAM

Belief in and commitment to freedom of thought and religion are recognized in international laws and the Universal Declaration of Human Rights. However, believing in human rights and having freedom of belief does not mean immunity of religion and faith from critical scrutiny. The same law that recognizes religious freedom also acknowledges the freedom to criticize religion. There is no contradiction between believing in religious freedom and engaging in comprehensive and simultaneous criticism of religion and faith.

The meaning of respecting human rights and being committed to the freedom of belief does not imply negligence to the influence of religious ideologies on people's lives. A community's citizens, religious or not, should be critics of the religion of a government that seizes power and suppresses the people. Therefore, shallow and biased analyses, filled with censorship and media standards that do not allow the expression of the role of religion in politics and society, are not real or reflective of the truth.

The Iranian revolution did not happen against Christian or Jewish governments or other ideologies. The people of Iran rose up against the Islamic government, a government that, according to its constitution, is supposed to be based on Islamic laws in all its decisions and regulations. However, for the past 44 years, the Islamic regime has established its foundations from the smallest imaginable issues to the most significant problems and dilemmas of the country, based on compliance and not being contradictory with the Islamic texts and the opinions of jurists. Therefore, the consequences and results of the events that have occurred in Iran are undoubtedly related to the religious authorities and Islamism.

Those who deny the relationship between government and religion or those who attempt to separate the government's actions from Islamic ideology have no reasonable justifications.

Their statements are driven by personal reasons and affiliations. Advocating for the immunity of religion in the face of atrocities is not an argument but rather an individual's desperate attempt to preserve their ideology, with no alternative solution other than grasping at any available pretext.

If someone has a personal interest or emotional connection to a religion, they do not have the right to sacrifice tangible reality for their personal inclinations. It's like a child who knows that their father is at fault in an incident, but in the moments of judgment and decision, sees him as faultless and innocent due to the father-child relationship, and the love and affection that exists between them, which prevents them from acknowledging the truth.

Human affections are one of the greatest cognitive biases that hinder understanding and perception of reality and proper judgment. It either distorts issues differently or, after understanding the truth, influences the person in a way that forces them to make incorrect judgments and analyses. Some individuals who claim that there is no relationship between Islam and the Islamic regime suffer from this kind of cognitive bias. In other words, due to their intense religious emotions and inclinations, they cannot or do not want to accept that religions, in the realm of governance, have had and continue to have negative and unacceptable consequences.

Individuals, especially those who have been involved in religious beliefs from childhood to adulthood, have undoubtedly established a stronger emotional bond with religion. This deeply rooted feeling prevents them from accepting the disastrous consequences of the role of religion in the Islamic government. Their words are understandable but not acceptable because the religious attachment they have toward their religion does not exist in others. The sense of belonging that has led them to consider their justifications as logical does not exist in many people. The whole efforts of some individuals are all about protecting their religion, but, with such behavior, they have sacrificed the truth and humanity for their personal biases.

They have made religion the foundation and essence of their personality and identity, and they deny or interpret anything incorrectly that contradicts that foundation in a different way.

If the Islamic regime has no relationship with Islam, then all Islamic governments likely do not have such a connection, too. But they are all derived from and manifestations of the essence of Islam, just in different ways. Each group considers others outside the core of their ideology. For example, Saudi Arabia, Pakistan, Afghanistan, Turkey, Qatar, and Iran all have governments with Islamic inclinations, and each considers itself the most Islamic and the others are farther from Islam. However, religion is a collection of existing interpretations and has a general influence that varies in intensity and weakness in different societies. Religion is not an external subject that is formed in a vacuum. The Mullahs have governed the country using Islamic thought in their Islamic regime. It is understandable if some individuals interpret religion differently from the regime, but their interpretation has no relevance to or impact on the reality that is prevailing in the country.

Essentially, the difference in religious perspectives of an individual living in a certain place of the world and the interpretation of the Islamic government does not hold any significance when criticizing the ideology of Islam. The subject is the Islam that exists in Iran, not the Islam that was made and pursued by some in their dreams and desires. Everyone has the right to understand Islam in all of its facets, but no one has the right to prevent others from criticizing religion or expressing the role that religion has in the government under the pretext of different interpretations. The fundamental problem is that Iran's Islamic government, which has legislation based on Islam, has resulted in a combination of religion and government. The events that have taken place in Iran are a direct result of the behavior of the Mullahs and their ideology of Islam.

With all these descriptions, this is the main question: Is the "Woman, Life, Freedom" revolution is anti-religion, anti-Muslim, or neither?

The conflict against the Islamic government is a battle against the integrity of the regime's structure, from regime officials to laws, and the nature of such a murderous apparatus.

The Iranian revolution is not a fight against an individual or an institution, but rather a multidimensional struggle that will change the foundation of governance and traditional religious mindset. Since the Islamic regime is not merely an authoritarian system, but a totalitarian and hegemonic regime, the meaning of fighting against a religious government is a battle against any law and structure that has formed and defined the Islamic government's nature.

The first point is that fighting against the Islamic government does not signify being anti-Muslim since being Muslim does not equate to supporting the government. Being Muslim does not mean being equal to the ruling ideology. Being Muslim does not mean being equivalent to a Mullah. Being Muslim does not mean being the oppressor. It is indeed correct and necessary to fight against them if certain Muslims are part of the governing power and suppress the people, but not because they are Muslim, rather it's because they are suppressors and killers. So, being a Muslim or not is neither the criterion for enmity nor friendship. It does not make a difference if the oppressor is Muslim or not a believer in religion. The criterion for enmity and friendship is the degree of individuals' proximity or distance to human rights, freedom, and justice.

One of the main principles and goals of Iranians in the "Woman, Life, Freedom" revolution is the very important concept of *freedom*, which includes individual and social freedoms. Who has the right to freedom and equality? Of course, all human beings do. Therefore, Muslims have the right to freedom and equality. In other words, the revolution against the Islamic government is also a revolution for the freedom of Muslims and the preservation of their rights. The slogan of freedom most definitely includes people who have different beliefs and diverse religious tendencies, including Christians, Jews, atheists, Muslims, Baha'is, and any other ideology and thought. Iranians are seeking to replace a system that recognizes the principles of religious freedom rather than privileging one group over another or one religion over another and, therefore, creating social inequality and public dissatisfaction. The Iranian revolution will also liberate Muslims from the clutches of oppressors and Mullahs. Muslims will undoubtedly be supported by the revolutionary and democratic people of Iran, and there will be no opposition to their free life.

Protecting the religious rights of citizens is among the criteria and fundamental principles of the freedom-seeking revolution of "Woman, Life, Freedom". If all members of society, from atheists to Muslims, were to engage in activities based on the common principles of the Universal Declaration of Human Rights, then each individual would act as defined by the freedom and rights of others. Differences will not be a cause for enmity and conflict. However, if an individual or group decides to eliminate or restrict others or attempts to violate the rights of citizens under the pretext that a particular religion is correct or respected, they will undoubtedly face the reaction of society. The struggle against the Islamic government in no way means opposition to Muslims. Many secular Muslims have participated in the "Woman, Life, Freedom" uprising.

Some of the parents of Iranian fighters are Muslim, and some of the individuals who were arrested and injured in the streets and protests were Muslims, but they did not believe in governmental and political Islam. Some of the deceased heroes and martyrs, who were Muslims and fought alongside secular individuals against the Islamic government in the "Woman, Life, Freedom" revolution, became symbols of freedom and bravery. The Iranian revolution is comprehensive and pluralist. For example, women from the province of Sistan & Baluchestan actively participated in gatherings and protests, even though they attended while wearing Islamic, or traditional Baloch, clothing. They chanted slogans of "Woman, Life, Freedom" or *regardless of being veiled or unveiled, moving toward the revolution.* Such occurrences were extraordinarily mesmerizing and full of beauty.

They nullified and neutralized all the false propaganda of the Mullahs and the terrorist Revolutionary Guards (Sepah).

Muslim women who chant slogans against the Islamic government, while wearing a veil or Islamic attire, expose the deception of the Islamic regime.

These women declare:

"As citizens of the country, we are not supernumerary forces of a group of traitorous tyrants who commit any crime and justify their actions under the pretext of the existence of Muslims and considering themselves legitimate ... while being Muslim, we are fighting against the Islamic government."

If the Islamic regime seeks to instill a fascist interpretation of the Iranian revolution, or if the authorities aim to create a general prejudice against Iranian freedom fighters, or if they have launched propaganda campaigns saying that if the democracy advocates came to power that would result in burning Muslims alive, their goal is nothing but to divide and generate fear among united and cohesive groups of the Iranian nation. This means that Mullahs have created divisions among the people as one of their defensive methods. They fear unity and harmony among the people, so their strategy in waging war against the Iranian nation is to break up and eliminate unity and send signals of discord. They want to turn the people into isolated and disconnected islands. The authorities and Mullahs have realized that they can no longer control and suppress the people, so they are attempting to create divisions and separations under the pretext of ethnic, religious, and linguistic differences. Words do not come out of their mouths unless they're of an unreal and deceptive nature.

Similar to the Russian government, the Islamic regime seeks to maintain its rule through widespread lying and organized massacres, but the Iranian people, in addition to disregarding the regime's lies about being anti-Muslim, have displayed a resolute and striking response on the streets.

Both veiled and unveiled women came together hand in hand and took to the streets to protest. They showed the most beautiful form of unity among the Iranian people. The joint protest of religious and non-religious individuals demonstrated the unity of the people and presented a democratic image of the Iranian revolution. On one hand, this act declared the position of secularists in solidarity with the religious people. And, on the other hand, it declared religious people's position against the principles and regulations of the Islamic government. In fact, the declaration of opposition against the Mullahs by Muslims living in Iran is extremely important and fundamental. The Islamic regime opportunistically exploits their beliefs and uses the existence of Muslim citizens to portray them as the defenders and supporters of the regime in Iranian society. In a situation where the regime has used Muslims for its legitimacy and authority, then their behavior will undoubtedly be highly effective.

The second point is that, due to the lived experience of Iranians under a religious government with an Islamic framework, it is normal that many Iranians have developed a non-aligned view toward Islamic ideologies. The number of individuals who do not have religious beliefs or don't consider religion is not important in their lives has greatly increased. But is it wrong or illegal to oppose Islamic ideologies? The issue is that every individual has the right of opposition. Just as Muslims do not accept Christian beliefs, atheists or non-religious individuals also do not accept Islamic ideologies. However, these oppositions do not imply enmity or hostility between secular Iranians and those who are religious. Instead, they fight against an illegitimate regime together, even with their differences, for each other's freedom on one front. In developed societies, differences and opposition are considered natural and a result of different perspectives. Similarly, if Iranians have different opinions about each other's ideas and views, it will by no means imply a confrontation with the religious people.

In such situations, there is a need to demonstrate our own democratic nature and behavior. If we strive for freedom and democracy, we must also be tolerant and accommodating of dissent. Therefore, opposition to Islam or Islamism is natural and the right of every Iranian citizen. Having opposition to Islam and expressing it in an isolated and suffocating society may seem unnatural or unusual to some people but giving special privileges for a particular religion and absence of freedom of expression are exactly what Iranians have risen against.

Many Iranian individuals have been imprisoned and killed, for years, for opposing religious ideologies – this opposition was their *right*. In a democratic society, dissent will have no cost, and every individual is free to express their opinions without fear or hesitation.

Reducing sensitivities and considering the right of others to think and speak differently, just as we consider it for ourselves, is an important factor in cultural and political development. Individuals with religious and non-religious beliefs must respect and acknowledge the right of others to dissent. Democratic people are united despite their differences, unlike nondemocratic people, who will not cooperate unless they conform to each other in a specific form. If many Iranians are not Muslim or do not have religious inclinations, it is not and should not be a sensitizing issue, as they are using their right to choose their personal beliefs. There has been a government in the lived experience of the Iranian people that made Islam the centerpiece of every one of its affairs. Therefore, opposition to a governmental Islam or opposition to Islamic ideas is an inevitable occurrence.

But these oppositions will have two prominent reasons:

1. to experience the implementation of religious laws, and
2. to gain greater knowledge of beliefs and religious laws.

Each of these two factors can be among the main reasons for the Iranian inclination toward secularism and modernity.

For example, if a group of Christians lives in a land where the rulers of that country are Jewish, and the Jewish government has brought the country into decline and collapse based on Jewish laws and has decided to eliminate or weaken Christians, then in this situation, it is normal for Christians to oppose Jewish thinking, when they are being oppressed. If some nongovernmental Jews have a different interpretation or another perception of their own faith, it will not be entered into the matter because the opposition of oppressed Christians in that land will be against the Jewish religion, which has turned into a source of legislation and injustice. In another example, some oppressed Christians may consider the entire structure of Jewish thoughts to be a fallacy, and this inclination means simultaneous opposition to the religious government and opposition to the essence of Judaism, both of which are part of their undeniable rights. The debate and conflict about the extent to which these oppressions are approved or not approved by religion is an intra-religious issue that will be subject to controversy and discussion.

Opposition to religion is the right of every Iranian, just as agreeing with religion is the right of every Iranian. The main point is that, in opposition and consent, there is no right for anyone to violate human rights for any reason. If the dominance of religion is generally in Middle Eastern societies for various reasons, the people of Iran do not want such dominance in politics or public culture. Religion should have clear boundaries, and if it does not, the disintegration of society is inevitable. The era of religious domination over culture and politics has passed as, in the current modern world, human life is the most vital and fundamental issue that exists and can be imagined. Anything that poses a threat and limitation to the citizen's lives and freedom must be controlled. The "Woman, Life, Freedom" slogan is a clear and secular message that has no relation to biased traditions and anti-human beliefs. Rather, it is a matter above ideology. This slogan is a shout for the Iranian people's transition from the dominance of ideologies. It is a subject that many ideologically influenced societies have a problem with, even in imagination, and sometimes choose the opposite path.

Can a discourse that goes beyond ideology, religion, and tradition attract religious people? The answer to this is that it depends on the perspective of a religious person toward the teachings of their religion. If they see religion as a personal matter and a matter of personal belief, they will be capable of perceiving a discourse that is beyond their religious teachings. That's because their being religious is not absolute and totalitarian.

However, if the people's religiosity is biased and dogmatic, they will oppose any discourse that goes beyond their beliefs because they seek all truth and absolute reality within their religion and faith. A significant portion of Iranian religious people also find secular and non-ideological concepts rational and logical. That is why many individuals who had beliefs in religion actively participated in and supported the "Woman, Life, Freedom" revolution. The revolution and the formation of a secular society should be supported by every group and tendency, whether religious or non-religious. In a free society, religious actions and rituals are carried out based on personal will and individual choice. However, in religious governments, certain factors, such as the environment, media, education system, and government interference in people's religiousness, play a destructive role. If religious beliefs and convictions derive from government interference, they are not the result of a religious person's thoughts but rather a product of political propaganda and indoctrination. Therefore, in a secular society, individuals' religiosity will be purer and based on their own choices.

On the other hand, in a society where religion is sold to people through imposition and force, religiosity loses its meaning because the compulsion eliminates any authenticity of human behavior. The criterion for evaluating human behavior is the individual's own will. A religious society that is based on compulsion undermines the personal values of the religious. Now if such imposition persists nationwide for decades, it will only result in discrediting the school or ruling ideology, and, naturally for many, such a religion will be unacceptable and inadmissible.

The opposition and negative perspective of some Iranians toward a religion or ideology that has caused them discrimination and injustice is normal. They consider it the cause of the ruin and destruction of the country and degraded lives. Some believers' affiliation to a religion should not obstruct the freedom of others to oppose that religion.

Opposing governmental Islam and the principles of Islam are both parts of individuals' rights. Disapproval of the hijab is a legitimate right for a woman who has endured mandatory hijab for decades or even for a woman who has not experienced such a situation. In fact, since the religious authorities have introduced this law as Islamic, there is no escape from disgust with a wrong and inhumane law. Some may argue that mandatory hijab is not a part of the religion!

The issue is that many claim it is part of the religion. With this description, should an Iranian citizen consider the disagreements of a group as the criteria for their perspectives? The fact that believers, even after hundreds of years, still do not know what the correct interpretation is of Islam is their own concern. The problem lies in the fact that the religion they believe in has multiple interpretations and is a citable statement for any group or faction.

The main issue is that many disasters that have occurred are the products of religious resources and the performance of religious authorities. It doesn't matter what interpretation is correct about true Islam. It has no significance in the fight against the Islamic government. Iranians are faced with a religion that is running the country and interpreted by the experts of that religion. Therefore, when a revolution occurs against the existing structure and ruling ideology, it is a revolt against a system that has caused the country to decline, against the Mullahs, against the political system, against political Islam, against the tradition of patriarchy, and against existing laws, including the constitution. During such a comprehensive revolution, some believers have prominent religious concerns and look at the future and the Iranian revolution with a sense of fear. I consider the feeling of fear or concern that some religious individuals have to be somewhat natural because new and different subjects mean stepping out of the previously known environment, which will create a sense of insecurity.

The subject is the process of transition from tradition to modernity, changing the nature of the old structure toward a new structure. Changes are often concerning, especially when fundamental changes occur. On the other hand, granting religious freedom equally may seem unusual and extraordinary to Muslims, especially Shia Muslims, due to their special privileges, compared to other believers in the Islamic regime. However, after the removal of the Islamic government, these special privileges will change, and everyone will be considered equal. Any religion that has special privileges and status will have to put it away and will be treated equally with all other beliefs within the framework of the law. The fact is that Shia Muslims and Shia Islam have been free to practice rituals and worship, and the new system is expected to provide support and legal rights from non-believers to Baha'is. This creates an implicit fear for some religious people to an understandable extent. But if the reason and intention is the desire to remove the rights of others and demand permanent extra support, it is not acceptable because religious and ideological discrimination will not have a place in a free and secular Iran.

The main cause of the fear of religious-concerned people is having an unclear perception and incorrect understanding of the concept of the Iranian revolution. While the continuation of the terrifying Islamic regime is definitely cause for concern, freedom and secularism are not. Without a doubt, in a democratic system, there will be no opposition or discrimination against religious individuals in the execution of religious and personal rituals. Citizens' personal opinions can be criticized but not attacked. However, if some individuals use religion as a tool for social behavior, like some Muslims who are currently hindering and opposing democracy in England and France, or religious extremists in Iran who are trying to eliminate the freedoms of others, then it is obvious that they should be stopped. Among Iranians, the issue of coercion and interference by others in personal lifestyles will eventually be thrown in the trash can of history.

Since religious people believe in using coercion to enforce their religious beliefs, they will be opposed to the Iranian revolution because those believers do not believe in the Universal Declaration of Human Rights. They do not believe in the freedom of others and oppose the principles of the Iranian revolution. They do not want the equality and security of others. In this case, the opposition of a religious believer to the Iranian revolution will not be of great importance because the principles of the revolution, which include freedom, human rights, and secular democracy, are not negotiable and can't be contradicted by individuals. Or some groups agree to overthrow the regime but oppose the establishment of secular democracy while respecting human rights. Some may want to replace the current Islamic regime with an Islamic Sunni government or establish a nationalist chauvinist government, both of which would be unacceptable. The essence and nature of governments require neutrality toward tendencies and religions. A state religion or extremist tendencies will undoubtedly not lead to public satisfaction but will serve as a pretext for suppressing minorities, while democracy, by a more evolved definition, is to protect the rights of minorities.

Therefore, the official religion and special privileges create social divisions. Religious and non-religious extremism inclinations will have no place in the secular and humanistic Iranian revolution. The "Woman, Life, Freedom" revolution is inherently secular. Secularism is based on the separation of religion and state, which is a popular belief among Iranians. I believe it is based on a philosophical secularism (with varying degrees of intensity) that exists in Iranian society to an extensive level. In the future of Iran, the existence of a religious government or an authoritarian political structure will not be publicly accepted.

According to the fundamental principle, nothing is more important than the lives and well-being of humans. Therefore, the security and worth of all citizens, regardless of their religious or ideological beliefs, should be respected. But any religious or non-religious person who plans to violate and infringe upon others' human rights and seeks to oppose the freedom and social security of citizens will be seen as someone who needs to be controlled. As it stands, individuals in Iran's current situation have established a religious government and ignored all the people's rights, making their lives a plaything for their meaningless goals. Such anti-human persons are the legitimate target of the comprehensive fight.

For Iran and Iranians, an event called religious governments or the dominance and influence of Mullahs and religion has come to an end. Islam, like any other religion, will be limited to personal beliefs and the relationship between individuals and God. Political Islam and interventionist Islam will have no place in Iran's future. The Iranian Revolution was born through the blood of the best and purest Iranians, and protecting the goals of these people is one of the most important duties of every Iranian. All religions and creeds, especially Islam, which have had specific influences in the country for various reasons, will be bound by fair laws and confined to their own boundaries and limits. Of course, limiting the influence of Islamic ideology will be difficult after its long period of unlimited freedoms, but, without a doubt, this will happen.

After experiencing religious governance, especially the Islamic one, it seems obvious to determine boundaries for the activities of religions in the social sphere. Everyone knows that, in some way, the disasters that religious influence brings to the political and legislative atmosphere. With such an approach, it is clear why the activities of religions, especially Islam, should be viewed from within a defined framework.

Of course, one should refer predominantly to Islam for three reasons:

1. The historical oppression that the people of Iran have endured from Mullahs and Islamists.
2. The Islamic government that the people have fought against has resulted in decades of many innocent deaths, injuries, and imprisonments.

3. I believe that Islamic extremism poses a greater threat than other beliefs, so it is obvious to associate greater caution with this greater threat.

Clearly, secular Muslims should not be annoyed with such a matter because they are also aware of the historical events that have affected the Iranian people in some way. And indifference toward injustice and oppression is not part of our criterion for judgment. The problem of understanding the oppression toward Iran and Iranians is not only related to secularists or other thinkers, but also to religious individuals who can understand the widespread historical oppression, by religious authorities, against their own people. Therefore, this religious individual is also aware of the direction of the discussed issue. This person, who opposes the Islamic government, can see the unbelievable impact that a government based on religious content has had on people's lives. Therefore, they take appropriate positions in response to events and understand potential future risks.

Islamism and Islamists are obliged and responsible for the current events in Iran. Their behavior is not something that has happened and been forgotten. It is ongoing and will continue to have repercussions. It's obvious that the sweetness of oppressive dominance through illegitimate power will result in bitter outcomes when it is time to take accountability.

This does not mean to discriminate against or be biased toward a specific religion. It means to seek justice. Protestants and Christians have not taken Iran and Iranians hostage, but Shia Muslims and Islamists have. As a result, my reaction and that of others toward Shia Islamism will be different from our reaction toward Protestantism or Orthodox.

If the reaction we have toward Shia Islamism is the same as we have toward Protestantism, then that is a sign of ignorance and moral unjust. Just as Europe's reaction during the Renaissance was not toward Islamism but toward the Catholic Church because the priests and religious sources of Catholicism were the oppressors and legitimizers of the kings and the usurpers of people's properties in Europe. Every idea is responsible for the implementation of its content. The useful and harmful consequences of ideas will determine the nature of the reactions. If a religion or ideology selfishly, and opportunistically, controls the public lives of human beings with its content, it should accept the consequences of such decisions rather than being silent in times of accountability and responsibility, as well as seek excuses and justifications.

Throughout history, the combination of religion and government has always led to inequality and division. This is the inevitable result of political religion because the philosophy and purpose of forming governments have no proper connection to the religion's content and purpose. Therefore, trying to link two completely unrelated subjects will result in the loss of both simultaneously. Combining religion and government leads to a hostile or unfriendly stance from people toward the religion of the government. While initially, religious people may be happy when their chosen religion is gaining power, ultimately, they find themselves confronted with a sort of self-made cage that they have voluntarily constructed and deprived themselves of their own independence. A clear example of such discontent is seen among Muslims, who form part of the Iranian population. In the early establishment of the Islamic government in Iran, many individuals who believed in religion and faith expressed joy and delight over such an event.

They were initially enthusiastic about the religion getting stronger, but such happiness quickly turned into disappointment and dissatisfaction, and even a number of the religious believers realized their mistake. They believed that if religion was mixed with the government, the situation would be improved, and more people would be inclined toward spirituality and God. This was the very point where they deviated from justice and fairness, as they sought to develop and promote Islamic beliefs by controlling and abusing the land's resources and violating the minds of adults and children. This opportunistic misconduct resulted in the opposite outcome. Not only did Islamism *not* strengthen in Iran, but the population became less religious. The compulsory hijab, which had been imposed on women, was abandoned, and even those who did believe in wearing it began to doubt their beliefs, causing the collapse of their religious convictions.

Mosques and places of worship have become empty to the extent that even Abolqasem Doulabi, the special representative of the president of the Islamic regime in religious affairs, admitted it: *"Out of 75,000 mosques in the country, 50,000 are closed, which is a tragedy that should be cried for."*

Establishing religious governments will not only inevitably face defeat and downfall but also lead to a decline in religious inclination. This point should be understood and accepted by a religious person. But because the outward display of religion, which is getting strong, is important and attractive to many believers, they ignore the consequences and implications of such a choice, ignoring the fact that a religious government means the responsibility of religion and religious persons for the shortcomings and problems. In the face of suffocation, people will blame the religion and religious authorities. In the face of economic and cultural problems, they will consider the basis and foundation of the religious system as the root of problems. Of course, the people are right and make the correct judgment.

Religion should not have a role in the management and design of political and social affairs. The revolution and process of modernization in Iran have also sought to separate religion from politics for this reason. Even though so many Iranians are believers, they can't validate the establishment of a religious government because they have already experienced the consequences of that kind of government and do not want it (to continue). Despite their diversity in beliefs, Iranians *are* united in overthrowing and destroying the Islamic regime.

Of course, the diversity of beliefs and different views among all people worldwide is natural. American and German societies, despite achieving modernity and having secular structures, have religious citizens who pursue their desired lives while preserving

rights and freedoms, and such inclinations have not done fundamental damage to secular democracies. Therefore, the existence
of religious Iranians does not imply the acceptance of a political
Islam or religious government, just as an American Christian,
Jewish, or Muslim person does not want a Christian, Jewish,
or Islamic government; but, rather, they think in a completely
secular manner (that religion does not have a place in government). Therefore, the existence of religious secularists does not
hinder the realization of secular democracy, just as nonbeliev-
ers and non-Muslims will not hinder the growth and freedom
of religious believers.

novum PUBLISHER FOR NEW AUTHORS

The publisher

He who stops getting better stops being good.

This is the motto of novum publishing, and our focus is on finding new manuscripts, publishing them and offering long-term support to the authors.
Our publishing house was founded in 1997, and since then it has become THE expert for new authors and has won numerous awards.

Our editorial team will peruse each manuscript within a few weeks free of charge and without obligation.

You will find more information about
novum publishing and our books on the internet:

w w w . n o v u m - p u b l i s h i n g . c o . u k